ECONOMIC DEVELOPMENT
AND STRUCTURAL CHANGE

Economic Development and Structural Change

EDITED BY I. G. STEWART

at the University Press
Edinburgh

© Edinburgh University Press 1969
EDINBURGH UNIVERSITY PRESS
22 George Square, Edinburgh
North America
Aldine Publishing Company
529 South Wabash Avenue, Chicago
85224 053 8
Library of Congress
Catalog Card Number 69-16014
Printed in Great Britain by
The Kynoch Press, Birmingham

Preface

This book contains the papers presented at an International Seminar on problems of Economic Development and Structural Change held by the Department of Economics in the University of Edinburgh from 7 to 10 April 1968.

The idea of having a Seminar at which academic, business and government economists could exchange observations on the prospects facing less-developed countries sprang from several sources of inspiration and support. In the first place, members of the Department of Economics had, with the financial assistance of the United States Department of Agriculture, been working on problems of structural change in West African countries, notably Ghana. Their work had previously (1964) led to a successful Seminar devoted to African primary products and international trading relations. At that time the United Nations Conference on Trade and Development had just held its first full-scale meeting in Geneva. In the early months of 1968 UNCTAD II, took place in Delhi, and although the event was not a happy one for the less-developed nations, this was nevertheless still an opportune time for a gathering of some forty economists to attempt a sympathetic appraisal.

It is doubtful whether these considerations by themselves would, however, have sufficed to get this Seminar off the ground. What really turned thought into deed was the friendly stimulus imparted by Mr Alan F. Peters and his colleagues at Shell International. That the Seminar took place successfully was in great measure due to the generous financial assistance made available in this way to the Department of Economics.

While the papers which follow range over a variety of topics, the underlying theme linking most if not all of them is an appraisal of 'structural changes' that are occurring or need to occur if the less-developed countries of Africa, Asia and Latin America are to improve their lot. The Opening Address on 'Trade, Education and Economic Development' put all who participated even further in Professor Myint's debt for directing attention to the fundamental issues in this context.

The task of organising the Seminar was shared by a number of colleagues in the Department of Economics and in the Centre of African Studies. The thanks of the participants in the meetings are

PREFACE

due to Professor A. J. Youngson who as Head of the Department and Dean of the Faculty of Social Sciences gave every encouragement to the venture. I should like, as Editor, to thank Mr Michael Allingham in the Department of Economics for his invaluable assistance, also Dr T. David Williams and Miss Grace Hunter in the Centre of African Studies, and Mrs M. Paton, Miss Jennifer Alsop and Miss Jessica Donoghue for their secretarial assistance in the Department of Economics.

Ian G. Stewart
Edinburgh, January 1969

Contents

Trade, Education and Economic Development

I should like to talk about certain broad issues of international trade and economic development. I shall try to show that there is a close interconnection between current discussions on trade and development and on education and development: that, in particular, a certain analogy can be drawn between the currently fashionable view that the 'foreign exchange gap' of the underdeveloped countries should be filled in order to enable them to sustain their import-substitution policy of economic development and the equally fashionable view that the underdeveloped countries should carry out 'crash' programmes in educational expansion in order to close their 'technological gap' with the advanced countries. I shall hope to show that both these views are vitiated by a common fault in reasoning, by the 'fallacy of misplaced concreteness'.

Let me start with international trade theory. Development economists tend to dismiss the theory of comparative costs as static and inadequate to cope with the problems of the underdeveloped countries. One of the reasons for this dissatisfaction is that the conventional theory of comparative costs is concerned with the 'direct' gains from trade and is strictly neutral between the desirability of expanding production for the export market or the domestic market. Starting from a given situation, the question whether more resources should be transferred to the export sector or the domestic sector should be decided strictly according to the given comparative costs. On the other hand, it is rare to find any development economists maintaining this neutral attitude to foreign trade and domestic production. They tend to be either for expanding export production or for expanding domestic manufacturing industry as the mainspring of economic development policy and they tend to speak of the 'dynamic' or 'indirect' effects beyond the 'direct' 'static' gains from international trade.

A full-scale discussion of the relative merits of the 'export-expansion' versus 'domestic-industrialisation' approach to development policy would have to range over a variety of issues, e.g. the economies of scale and the size of the market, technical complementarities and external economies, the long-term prospects of the world

B

market demand for primary exports from the underdeveloped countries and so on. I have discussed some of these issues elsewhere;[1] but for my present purpose, I should like to focus attention on the 'educational' element in this controversy. I should like to suggest that, when stripped of its complications, the crux of this controversy consists in a clash between two different views about the type of education which economic policy should seek to promote in the underdeveloped countries in order to accelerate their rate of economic development.

There are various arguments which can be advanced in support of the view that the underdeveloped countries are likely to enjoy rapid economic growth by reducing their existing network of controls over foreign trade and investment and by allowing the world market forces to transform their internal economic structure according to their potential comparative advantage. But when hard-pressed, those who favour this 'outward-looking' approach to development policy would probably fall back on their fundamental belief in the powerful 'educative effect' of the contact with the outside world on the underdeveloped countries. They would say that 'economic development' is a foreign and outside thing for the underdeveloped countries and that if these countries really desire economic development they have somehow or other to open themselves to the stimulus of outside economic forces instead of insulating their economies from them. The advocates of the 'outward-looking' approach would then go on to emphasise the enormous educative effect of keeping an underdeveloped country open and receptive to new wants, new activities, new methods of economic organisation from abroad.

The belief in the 'educative effect' of an open economy is nothing new and can be traced back to the writings of the classical economists, particularly John Stuart Mill. Similarly, when we examine the arguments for promoting economic development through the protection of domestic industry, they also turn out to be based ultimately on an educational argument. The belief that manufacturing industry is somehow more educative than agriculture was first advanced by Friedrich List, and H. W. Singer sums up the modern interpretation of this belief very well when he writes that manufacturing industries 'provide the growing points for increased technical knowledge, urban education and the dynamism and resilience that goes with urban civilisation, as well as the direct Marshallian external economies'.[2]

Ultimately, then, we are left with two rival theories of education for economic development. How far can we adjudicate between these rival theories of educational sociology? It seems to me that the economist has a great deal to say towards obtaining a correct perspective on this question before venturing into sociology.

The first thing to be said is that it is misleading and inappropriate to identify 'industrialisation' in the sense relevant for economic development with manufacturing industry in the narrow sense. Economic development consists in the growth of national output as a whole and in the expansion of the various sectors which make up this total output. 'Industrialisation' in the broader sense relevant for economic development should therefore include not only manufacturing industry but also the creation of social overhead capital such as transport, and communications, irrigation, power, etc. and, above all, the 'industrialisation' of agriculture in the sense of applying modern science and technology to raise agricultural productivity.

The failure to appreciate this broader concept of 'industrialisation' and the attempt to identify it with manufacturing industry in the narrow sense is the root cause of the 'fallacy of misplaced concreteness' in current theorisings about promoting economic development through 'import substitution' of manufactured consumers' goods.

If we define industrialisation solely as the setting up of manufacturing industry, then 'capital goods' are automatically identified with durable machinery required by the modern manufacturing sector. Since most underdeveloped countries are too small and too economically backward to be able to set up machine-producing industries successfully, we have the generally accepted doctrine that import-substitution should start from or be confined to manufactured consumers' goods. Since 'capital goods' in the sense of durable machinery cannot be produced domestically, the 'capital requirements' for economic development are translated into 'foreign exchange requirements'. The foreign exchange requirements are calculated on the basis of fixed technical coefficients between foreign inputs and domestic output. This type of calculation tends to emphasise the purely technological relations to the exclusion of the economic problem of making the best use of the scarce resources. We are asked to accept the existence of the import-substitution industries as *given* and are asked to confine ourselves to the notion of 'import requirements' which would follow purely as the engineering or technological consequence of operating them at full capacity or of maintaining the existing tempo of import substitution. Given the desired target rate of expansion in output and the fixed technical coefficients between foreign inputs and domestic output, the foreign exchange requirements for that rate of growth are projected. Comparing this with the projected foreign exchange receipts from exports (and international aid) we then have the size of the 'foreign exchange gap' to be filled up by an increase in international aid.

As you know, this type of import-substitution approach emphasising the 'foreign exchange gap' of the underdeveloped countries has gained considerable vogue since the first UNCTAD. I believe that it is open to a number of serious objections.

(i) If we accept that 'industrialisation' relevant for economic development should be defined broadly in terms of the growth of national output as a whole, then we should be concerned with the capital requirements not only for the manufacturing sector but also for social overhead investment and the agricultural sector. When we consider the nature of investment inputs required in these two latter sectors, it becomes very questionable whether 'capital goods' can be narrowly identified with durable machinery and whether it can be presumed that the potential comparative costs of the underdeveloped countries would always lie in the direction of import substitution of consumers' goods and not of the investment goods.

To begin with, at the earlier stages of economic development which characterise the underdeveloped countries, we should expect the capital requirements of social overhead capital and agriculture to be quantitatively more important than the capital requirements in the form of durable machinery by the manufacturing sector. The experiences of the advanced countries tend to support this. Kuznets pointed out that, during the second half of the nineteenth century, the share of producers' equipment in the total capital formation of the major advanced countries was as low as a fifth rising to over a third only during the recent decades. The rest of capital formation was in 'construction' both residential and for social overhead capital. [3]

Now social overhead capital, including irrigation and land improvement activities, essentially consists in construction which has to be done on the spot as distinct from machinery which is imported in a prefabricated form. While construction work may require some machinery, it requires to a much larger extent two other forms of input which offer promising scope for import substitution. First, it requires materials such as cement, brick, tiles, etc. which, because of weight and bulk and heavy transport costs, offer a natural protection to domestic production. The domestic manufacture of tubings for irrigation purposes in Pakistan is a notable example of this type of import substitution of investment goods. Second, even more fundamentally, construction work means putting a large number of workers to produce future output as distinct from present output: that is to say, before the work of these people yields consumable goods, they have to be supported by a 'subsistence fund' during the waiting period.

We are therefore back in the classical notion of capital as 'advances to labour' in the form of the 'subsistence fund'. It is my argument that in the underdeveloped countries this classical notion of capital as the 'subsistence fund' is of greater relevance than the modern concept of capital as durable machinery. If we accept that food is capital, then agriculture becomes a major investment-goods producing industry! Now a number of underdeveloped countries are having to import food and agricultural materials due to backward agriculture and population pressure. Thus an increase in domestic agricultural production can offer a considerable scope for 'import substitution' which would substantially contribute to the 'capital requirements' for economic development by enlarging the subsistence fund to maintain workers engaged in the construction of capital goods. Thus, Lockwood, in his well-known study of Japanese economic development, speaks of 'the general truth that the real capital assets required in various forms of economic growth must be largely produced at home'. [4]

(ii) We can go a step further to free ourselves from the 'fallacy of misplaced concreteness' which defines 'capital goods' and 'consumers' goods' according to their intrinsic physical properties and not according to the use they are put to in a given economic situation. If food can be regarded as 'capital goods' in the underdeveloped countries, what about the cheap imported consumers' goods which play the vital role of 'incentive goods' in many peasant economies of Asia and Africa? It seems to me that where the expansion of peasant agricultural production has been discouraged in spite of the availability of land and other physical inputs, because the highly protected domestic manufacturing industries cannot offer consumers' goods to the peasants on attractive terms, the freer importation of cheap incentive consumers' goods may be more to the purpose in encouraging the expansion of agricultural production than the importation of technical inputs which the peasants may not have the incentive to use. In this case I do not see why incentive consumers' goods should not be treated as 'inputs' to agriculture on the same footing as other technical inputs. This is the opposite of the currently fashionable view which stresses the statistical fact that since many underdeveloped countries are only importing machines and other technically required inputs but no consumers' goods from abroad, there is no further scope for cutting 'inessential imports.' In some of the underdeveloped countries, where domestic industries catering for luxury consumption by the urban classes have been encouraged to grow because of ineffective taxation and a desire to possess 'sophisticated' industries, it does not require much penetration to see that a considerable proportion of the so-called 'capital goods' and 'essential' inputs merely serve to satisfy luxury consumption inside the country.

(iii) Finally, the most serious objection that can be raised against the currently fashionable type of import-substitution approach is that it obscures the fundamental economic problem of choice. This problem is most clearly appreciated when we start from a given and limited amount of scarce resources, including foreign exchange receipts from exports and aid, available to a country and focus attention on the comparative advantage of using these resources among the alternative uses. In our setting, an underdeveloped country may be looked upon as having to face the problem of choice in two stages: first, how to convert the available domestic savings into 'capital goods' and second, how to use these 'capital goods' to obtain the final consumers' goods. At each stage, there is a choice between the 'direct' method of domestic production and the 'indirect' method of international trade. Thus, 'capital goods' can be either produced at home or imported from abroad; in the latter case, the foreign exchange to pay for them would have to be made available (leaving out aid) either by cutting down other imports or by cutting down domestic expenditure and shifting the resources thus released into export production. Similarly, having obtained the 'capital goods', the consumers' goods can be either produced directly at home or acquired indirectly in exchange for exports by using the 'capital goods' to produce exports.

Current thinking on import substitution implicitly identifies 'capital goods' with complex and sophisticated machinery which the underdeveloped countries have no choice but to import from abroad. But having obtained the 'capital' goods, current thinking implicitly assumes that it will always be preferable for the underdeveloped countries to use the 'capital goods' to produce consumers' goods directly at home instead of using the 'capital goods' to produce exports and acquire the consumers' goods indirectly through trade. I have been trying to show that, on a broader and more relevant definition of 'industrialisation' and 'capital goods', neither of these presumptions stand up to scrutiny and that there is a considerable case for taking the opposite view. But my objection at this point is not only that the currently fashionable import-substitution approach makes wrong economic judgments, but also that the habit of thought it engenders tends to push the whole economic problem of choice into the background and with it the necessity of making any explicit economic judgments whatsoever. The habit of assuming the existing import-substitution industries or the current tempo of import-substitution to be *given*, and inquiring only into the foreign exchange requirements of their continued operation, means that the problem of deciding which of the import-substitution industries are 'economic' and which are 'uneconomic' is relegated to the background. Instead of the economic problem of making the most of scarce resources, we are simply left with the technological problem of trying to run the existing industries at full capacity. But the central problem facing these industries is how to improve their efficiency and lower their costs. Their costs are made up of two components: the foreign exchange costs and domestic costs. In so far as they import machinery and other inputs at competitive world market prices, the reason for their high costs cannot be found in the foreign exchange component of their costs but in the domestic component. Yet the constant harping on the foreign exchange requirements of these import-substitution industries distracts attention from the vital domestic component of their costs which can make or mar their future development.

I can now draw the analogy between current thinking on promoting economic development through import-substitution and through educational expansion. Both are examples of the 'missing-component' approach. Import-substitution starts from a given target rate of growth which it is desired to achieve. Then, on the assumption of fixed technical coefficients between foreign inputs and domestic output, the foreign exchange requirements for the target rate of growth is estimated. Similarly, the theoretical model behind current discussions about education and skilled manpower planning starts from an autonomously given target rate of economic growth. It then assumes that there are fixed technical coefficients between various educational inputs and the national output. Thus the number of skilled people of various categories required to sustain a given rate of growth is estimated. The role of the educational system is to perform the passive function of filling the gap in the skilled manpower requirements, to achieve the target rate of growth as distinct from the active function of raising the possible rate of growth.

This notion of education and skills as the 'missing component' of economic development is reasonable enough in many underdeveloped countries immediately after their political independence. Then there were obvious gaps in skilled manpower created by the departure of expatriates in the various branches of the administrative and technical services. Sometimes the skills required were fairly specific and whole departments might not be able to function for lack of a few 'key' men. The situation then approximated to the assumption of fixed technical coefficients and it was obviously important for the underdeveloped countries to train their nationals quickly to fill these gaps. But since then the situation has changed. In the same way as most underdeveloped countries have passed through the 'easy phase' of import substitution, they have also passed through the easy phase of job redistribution from the expatriates to their own nationals. From now on, the rate of expansion in new jobs in skilled occupations must largely depend on the general rate of economic growth itself. In the meantime, as the result of the 'crash programmes' in education, the schools and universities in many underdeveloped countries are producing large numbers of fresh graduates at much faster rates than their general rate of economic growth. Thus there is a real danger, already familiar in many Asian countries, of growing unemployment among the educated classes which adds fuel to the fire of 'the revolution of rising expectations'. Here again there are similarities with import substitution. The process of rapid import-substitution in the underdeveloped countries tends to create excess capacity in the newly-built factories in spite of the heavy protection given to their products: this surplus of certain durable forms of capital goods tends to co-exist with a shortage of circulating capital in the form of food supply, inventories of all sorts and above all 'foreign exchange' which is the most liquid form of circulating capital. Similarly, educational expansion has created excess capacity in certain categories of 'human capital' in the form of university graduates, some of them with highly specialist technical qualifications. Yet, in the midst of growing graduate unemployment, there seems to be a genuine shortage of skilled people required for economic development, from competent people at the middle levels of skills to able entrepreneurs and civil servants at the top.

I would suggest that this similar outcome is basically due to the wrong allocation of resources resulting in the creation of wrong pieces of capital equipment, whether material or human, which cannot be economically absorbed into the existing productive structure of the underdeveloped countries. The underdeveloped countries are, for various reasons such as national prestige, easy victims to the lure of gleaming modern factories and imposing university buildings. But this tendency to make a fetish of the tangible outward symbols of economic development has also been encouraged by the 'fallacy of misplaced concreteness'. The import-substitution approach mistakenly identifies 'industrialisation' with the setting up of manufacturing industry in the narrow sense. Similarly, the advocates of 'crash programmes' in education mistakenly identify the general improvement in education, skills and training required for economic development with formal education in the narrow sense to be produced by the universities and technical colleges. I shall argue that formal education forms only a part and perhaps not the most important part of education in the broader sense relevant for economic development; and that ultimately the improvement in the economic competence of the mass of people in the underdeveloped countries will largely depend on the 'educative' influence of the whole economic environment in which they live.

But even in the sphere of formal education, there are certain biases and distortions in the educational programmes of most under-developed countries which can be attributed to the 'fallacy of mis-placed concreteness'. First, there is a bias in favour of producing too many university graduates and too few people at the middle level of skills, reinforced by top-heavy salary structures in favour of the graduates. Thus, many underdeveloped countries are acutely short of people to fill jobs at middle levels of skills while suffering from a relative glut of university graduates. Second, there is a bias in favour of producing graduates with specialist training in some applied branch of technology as against the general arts and science gradu-ates. Now this attempt to produce 'technical experts' equipped with highly specific types of 'technical know-how' is reasonable so long as there are clearly defined gaps in the skilled manpower require-ments of a country into which the 'missing components' can be fitted like pieces of a jig-saw puzzle. But after these gaps have been filled, the attempt to produce specialist technicians without any clear notion where they are to be fitted into the existing production structure increases the risk of wasteful creation of wrong pieces of 'human capital'. This can be seen in the growing number of students from the underdeveloped countries who have pursued highly specialist studies in applied technology in the advanced countries, only to find that their training and skills are too specifically adapted to the economic conditions of these countries to be usable when they return home. This can also be seen in the growing unemployment among the graduates of engineering colleges in some Asian coun-tries, such as India and Burma. Finally, there is the seeming paradox of a genuine shortage of capable entrepreneurs and civil servants side by side with inability to create a sufficient number of new jobs for the army of fresh graduates pouring out of the university. But considering the magnitude of the 'explosion' in the number of university students in most underdeveloped countries and their acute shortage of teachers, this is perhaps not altogether surprising. The rapid expansion of universities tends to lower academic standards both among the students and the teachers and, faced with large overcrowded classes, the teachers are in no position to select the more promising students and give them special attention. Thus it seems to me that the really crippling cost of the 'crash programmes' in education is to be reckoned in terms of the wastage of human re-sources: the more gifted students who could have developed into capable entrepreneurs and administrators have been prevented from realising their full potentialities by being crowded out by their less gifted fellows. [5]

Let me now turn to the broader concept of education in the sense of the 'educative' influence of the economic environment as a whole on the people of the underdeveloped countries. I cannot enter in any detail into the various ways in which the economic environment including the system of economic 'signals' and incentives can affect the economic behaviour of the people of the underdeveloped countries, their ability to make rational economic decisions and their willingness to introduce economic changes. All I can hope to do is to bring out some aspects of this subject sharply by returning to the question I have raised initially: namely, how to assess the rival claims of the 'educative effect' of the open economy and the 'educative effect' of manufacturing industry.

The answer which suggests itself at this stage is to consider the 'opportunity cost' in educational terms of free trade and protectionist policies in the present setting of the underdeveloped countries. To the protectionist, it is unsatisfactory for the underdeveloped countries to adopt free trade on the basis of the given comparative costs as determined by their existing level of skills. To pursue a free trade policy is therefore to miss the opportunity of improving the skills of the people through the process of learning-by-doing afforded by the protection of the 'infant industry'. To the free trader, the opportunity cost of protection to the underdeveloped countries is the insulation of their economies from the stimulus of the outside economic forces transmitting new wants, techniques and new methods of economic organisation. Now, so long as we are concerned with protecting carefully selected individual 'infant industries' while permitting free trade in the rest of the economy, it is difficult to say which way the net educational effects would go. The positive educative effect of learning-by-doing would have to be weighed against the possible negative educative effect on the entrepreneurs of a sheltered monopolistic market provided by the protection.

But current thinking on import substitution is concerned not merely with protecting individual 'infant industries', one at a time. It insists that the 'infant industry' argument for protection should be extended to cover the whole of the 'infant' manufacturing sector of the underdeveloped countries or even that the entire 'infant economy' of the underdeveloped countries should be insulated and protected from the pressures and disturbances of the external economic forces. Moreover, in a majority of the underdeveloped countries, this insulation is done not merely by tariffs and subsidies, but by a network of economic controls, ranging through quantitative import controls, price controls of agricultural products both for the domestic urban market and for the export market and controls on foreign investment and remittances. In this setting, I am inclined to believe that, leaving aside the wastages through misallocation of resources, the negative educative effects of this general insulation of the economy required to support a wholesale programme of import substitution is likely to outweigh its possible positive educative effects.

First, the typical modern manufacturing industry in the under-developed countries tends to adopt high capital-intensive techniques embodying sophisticated technology. It does so, not only for prestige reasons, but also because it has to pay high wages to its workers belonging to the politically powerful urban labour pressure groups and because it is in the privileged position of being permitted to import its capital equipment at official exchange rates in a situation where the domestic currency is highly overvalued through inflation. Thus, from the educational point of view, the modern manufacturing sector in the underdeveloped countries is in danger of growing into an 'enclave' employing only a small proportion of its labour force and having to employ a large number of foreign technical experts required by the sophisticated technology. In terms of educational impact there is much to be said in favour of encouraging the more labour-intensive small scale industries using simpler technology which requires a smaller technological gap to be bridged by the people of the underdeveloped country. Second, the import-substitution policy as currently practised generally entails keeping down the price offered to the agricultural producers. This is done either to keep down the cost of living for the urban workers; or to collect the funds to be invested in the manufacturing sectors as in the case of the state marketing boards in some of the Asian and African peasant export economies. In either case, the lack of incentive to the agricultural producers not merely discourages them from expanding output but what is more important, discourages them from adopting new methods to raise agricultural productivity. Finally, there are the well-known 'perverse' educative effects exerted by the foreign exchange controls over the indigenous entrepreneurs of the underdeveloped countries. Typically they find it more profitable to divert their energy and ingenuity from the task of raising productivity and efficiency to the task of procuring the necessary import licences, by hook or by crook, and exploiting the loopholes in government regulations. Clearly, such perverse educational effects are not likely to be remedied by 'crash programmes' in formal education.

To sum up: current thinking on import substitution and educational expansion has been vitiated by the habit of starting from a given target rate of economic growth and by concentrating on the purely technical problem of supplying the 'missing components' of durable capital goods and skills required to fulfil that rate of growth on the basis of fixed technical coefficients between these technically necessary inputs and total output. This has obscured the basic economic problem of allocating the available resources efficiently in the formation both of material and human capital so as to raise the rate of economic growth. This confusion between the 'technical' and the 'economic' problems is closely connected with the 'fallacy of misplaced concreteness' which narrowly identifies 'industrialisation' and 'education' relevant for economic development with manufacturing industry and the expansion of formal educational facilities. Once we free ourselves from this habit of thinking, it would seem that the underdeveloped countries can facilitate a more efficient import-substitution process according to their potential comparative advantage and can create an economic environment with a more favourable 'educative effect' for economic development by relaxing their existing network of controls over international trade and by permitting the outside economic influences to transform their economic structure. This policy of inducing 'structural change' for economic development by encouraging the flexibility and adaptability of the internal economic structure to the changing world market forces may be contrasted with the current policy of imposing 'structural change' to fulfil target rates of growth on the basis of fixed technical coefficients. I have no doubt that as economic development proceeds, the underdeveloped countries will find themselves with an expanding manufacturing sector and with a large number of highly trained specialists and technicians. But I suspect that the manufacturing industries and the specialists which will have grown up in the process of efficient adaptation to changing world market forces will not be the same as the manufacturing industries and specialist technicians which are now brought into being by the import-substitution programmes and the 'crash' programmes for educational expansion.

Notes and references

1 Cf. my paper 'International Trade and the Developing Countries' read at the 3rd Congress of the International Economic Association on the 'Future of International Economic Relations', Montreal, September 1968. I have used some of the materials from that paper in a condensed form in this talk.
2 H. W. Singer *International Development: Growth and Change* (New York 1964) pp. 164–5.
3 S. Kuznets *Modern Economic Growth: Rate, Structure and Spread* (New Haven 1966) p. 257, and table 5. 6.
4 W. W. Lockwood *The Economic Development of Japan* (Princeton 1965) ch. 5, p. 243.
5 Cf. my paper 'The Universities of Southeast Asia and Economic Development' *Pacific Affairs* Summer 1962.

A.I.MACBEAN

Foreign Trade Aspects of
Development Planning

It is a widely held view that the less developed countries are peculiarly dependent upon foreign trade and that this raises serious problems for them in both short and long-term economic planning.[1] Their stability and growth would appear to be dependent upon the behaviour of export markets which are outside their control. Moreover the behaviour of these markets for their main exports is thought to be highly unstable in the short-run and growing at a relatively slow pace in the long. At the same time attainment of 'acceptable rates of growth' is generally assumed to require imports to grow at rates faster than the average rate of growth of GNP and in a reasonably stable manner. As a consequence of these assumptions development planning in many LDCs has concentrated on reducing their dependence upon trade by emphasising policies of import substitution at home while seeking increased foreign exchange resources through aid, foreign investment, support for the prices of primary exports and trade preferences for processed exports, in international fora.

The question of short-term instability in exports and its effects on LDCs has been treated at some length elsewhere[2]. In this paper it is the long-term issues which form the main concern though economic planning can seldom afford to neglect the short-term. Long-term plans should be flexible enough to accommodate deviations from the trend values of projected variables. However, the premise that LDCs are in general exceptionally dependent on international trade in a quantitative sense is relevant to both the short and the long-term problems and is of doubtful validity. Calculated average ratios of foreign trade to national income are lower for a large sample of LDCs (52) than for a sample of developed countries (17)[3]. Kuznets[4] and Michaely[5] present data which indicate that LDCs are no more involved in foreign trade than advanced countries. The quantitative importance of exports relative to expenditure on investment and government expenditure appears to be significantly related to the size of nations, but not to whether they are developed or underdeveloped.[6]

Despite the lack of support for the special quantitative importance

of trade there may be sound reasons for supposing trade relationships to play a more important part in the development prospects of
LDCs than in advanced countries. Imports may have a greater
strategic role to play in domestic capital formation, in supplying
current inputs into existing manufacturing industries and in providing incentive goods. The first of these has figured prominently in
recent UN literature.[7] In the 'gap analyses' of economic models used
in planning,[8] and in S.B.Linder's new book, *Trade and Trade Policy
for Development*, both of the first two types of imports are treated as
the main constraint on the economic growth of those LDCs which
have started on the path of industrialisation.

The UN view implies a relatively fixed relationship between capital
goods imported and total imports, between imported capital goods
and domestic investment and between investment and increments of
national output. In fact *changes* in the first two ratios have been
significantly related to rates of growth of fixed capital formation in
developing countries. Countries with a high rate of growth of fixed
capital formation have tended to increase the proportion of capital
goods to total imports and to decrease the proportion of imports to
domestic investment.[9] Far from showing stability, incremental gross
capital/output ratios have shown a great deal of fluctuation in
developing countries.[10] Gap estimates predicted on the stability of
these three relationships stand upon very shaky foundations indeed.

The real challenge to neo-classical trade theory and its free trade
policy implications comes from the work of the writers cited in
footnote 8. Most of the other arguments for protection in the LDCs
can be accommodated in neo-classical theory. The 'infant industry'
argument depends largely on anticipation of the future development
of the comparative cost structure of the LDC. The terms of trade
argument for tariffs is unlikely to be important for an individual
LDC because the relevant price elasticities for its own exports and
imports are likely to be high. For LDCs as a group, acting in concert,
the possibility of shifting the commodity terms of trade in their
favour may well be a possibility, but would require the consent of
the rich countries if it were to avoid inflicting serious damage on all
through their adoption of retaliatory measures. Even if economic
welfare would in principle be improved by optimum tariffs the
practical difficulties of selecting the correct levels would seem in-
superable. Second best arguments for protection based upon distortions in the existing price structure would also be regarded as
minor qualifications of comparative cost theory. Choice of the
tariffs which would correct these price distortions and thus enable
achievement of an optimum resource allocation could also be considered to be so fraught with difficulties and risks of disadvantageous

side effects as to render such a policy impracticable.[11] Despite acknowledgment of these three qualifications the basic policy recommendation of orthodox trade theory remains one of free trade. Nevertheless, most LDCs are heavily protectionist. When theory and practice conflict so drastically it is incumbent upon the would-be-planner to re-examine his tools.

Staffan Linder's book[12] provides an extremely interesting rationale for at least some of the protectionist policies of some developing countries. It embraces the foreign exchange gap analyses of the Chenery genre and fits them into a more general theory of the relationship between trade and growth in countries in the process of industrial development.

The main points of his analysis can be summarised as:
1. There are certain types of goods essential to industrial investment which most LDCs cannot produce for themselves. One might say that their comparative disadvantage in producing many capital goods was near infinity.
2. In addition to these needs for new fixed capital formation there are replacement and maintenance imports which are essential to the continued operation of existing plant. There may be certain other raw material or intermediate goods which are also necessary and impossible to produce locally for some considerable time.

Conceptually there are these two types of imports which are required: (i) for expansion, (ii) for full capacity operation of existing plant. Both are *required* imports for the attainment of a desired rate of growth which is presumed to be within the administrative, technical and savings capacity of the economy.

$$M_r = M_1 + M_2 \quad \text{where } M_r = \text{required imports}$$
$$M_1 = \text{expansion imports}$$
$$M_2 = \text{maintenance imports}$$

Without M_2 the economy cannot operate at a sufficiently high level of national output to translate planned into actual savings. Without M_1 the savings cannot be turned into the investment needed for growth of capacity.

If there is an attempt to increase investment then with a given import capacity (exports plus autonomous capital inflow) M_1 will increase reducing foreign exchange available for M_2. This will result in lowered capacity utilization, lowered national output and frustrated savings.

The third assumption underlying this analysis is that foreign exchange receipts cannot be increased. The Prebisch view of stagnant demand for LDC exports is accepted. In addition to this Linder argues that the absolute level of productivity in manufactured exports may be so low that the value added in the production of exports may be negative; the cost of imported inputs may exceed the foreign exchange receipts for their sale.[13] Depreciation of the exchange rate will, in this case, give no assistance to manufactured exports. Reasons for the low absolute level of productivity stem from Linder's 'theory of representative demand'.[14] This states that a country becomes relatively more efficient at producing the kinds of manufactures for which there is a large internal market. The domestic demand stimulates inventors and businessmen into acquiring the best techniques and organization for satisfying these demands. The production functions for these particular goods will involve lower opportunity costs for them than for goods which are not typically in great demand in that economy. The chief determinant of the pattern of demand is the level of per capita income, consequently the pattern of demand will be very different in LDCs from that existing in the rich industrialised nations. It then follows that the production functions within LDCs for the production of the types of manufactures demanded in advanced countries will be relatively very inefficient. 'Owing to lack of foreign demand the developing countries therefore cannot export those manufactures they are most efficient at producing. Generally speaking, they are reduced to trying to export manufactures with which they are unfamiliar to markets of which they have no experience'.[15] Linder cites evidence on the difficulties LDCs find in marketing their exported manufactures.[16]

Linder sums up the general exporting difficulties of LDCs as (i) an export maximum for primary products, set by inelastic foreign demand and/or by decreasing marginal productivity, and (ii) severe limits on exports of manufactures to rich countries set by a low absolute level of productivity and the need for imported inputs for the kinds of goods which are acceptable to consumers in rich countries.

He concludes that those LDCs which have set out upon the path of industrial development inevitably find themselves constrained by an export maximum which exceeds the import minimum required for 'acceptable growth' combined with full utilization of existing industrial capacity. The orthodox answers to a balance of payments deficit will not work. Depreciation of the exchange rate will not expand demand for the primary exports because the price elasticities of demand are in general less than unity while their production is characterised by dimishing returns. Nor will it enable increased exports of the kinds of manufactures which they may be able to sell to advanced countries because devaluation raises the cost of the imported inputs essential to expanding such exports. Depreciation will only correct the balance of payments gap by reducing required imports and thus cutting back a more than proportional amount of expansion directed investment or by reducing utilization of existing manufacturing capacity. If the pursuit of orthodox adjustment measures cannot ensure simultaneous domestic and balance of payments equilibrium one of the basic assumptions of comparative cost theory is invalidated. It would no longer necessarily be true that free trade would maximise national economic welfare for the allocational improvements effected by freer trade could be outweighed by the losses caused by reductions in the employment of productive factors.

A further implication of the exchange gap theory which is of great interest to both aid donors and aid recipients is that any capital inflow forms not merely a supplement to domestic saving and investment but has a leverage effect on income and domestic capital formation. It enables a country which would otherwise be constrained by lack of required imports to put factors of production to work which would have been idle and to realize planned savings which would otherwise have been frustrated. 'Through this leverage effect, trade can be characterized as a super-engine of growth rather than as a mere engine of growth.'[17] Linder's formulation of foreign exchange gap analyses is of great interest as a powerful critique of neo-classical trade theory. It clearly has important implications for economic planning if the hypotheses which it advances are sound in principle and if the assumptions fit the situations of many LDCs.

Linder himself excludes a considerable number of LDCs from his analyses on the grounds that they are backward, depend entirely on primary exports, have large subsistence sectors and little or no industry. Countries where there is at least a prima facie case for the existence of foreign exchange gaps are those which have a developing manufacturing sector of reasonable size which is attempting to export to rich countries, and with foreign exchange receipts which are not buoyant. Such conditions would exclude a number of countries. Most of the oil and a number of other mineral exporting countries, for example, have been accumulating foreign exchange reserves for some time. India, Pakistan, Brazil, Colombia, Mexico and Chile could reasonably be put forward as countries where shortage of foreign exchange may be retarding economic growth. On the other hand most African countries could be excluded. Lack of absorptive capacity including ability to generate domestic savings seem much more important problems for most of them at present.[18] Clearly the number of LDCs which seem likely to fit the model is small. Nevertheless they contain a major portion of the population of the 'Third World' and a theory which helped to explain their difficulties would be very valuable. Moreover, the situation depicted by the Linder model may represent a stage through which most

LDCs will pass in the course of economic development. Prima facie the model is relevant and important. Symptoms consistent with it are displayed by several important LDCs. The question remains whether these symptoms stem from the causes which the theory outlines or whether other explanations which are consistent with orthodox theory fit the facts better.

Required imports

Linder's import minimum depends on much the same assumptions as the UN gap analyses criticised above: fixed factor proportions, inflexible composition of imports and an inflexible relation between imports and investment, and imports and existing capacity output. These assumptions deny the influence of costs and prices on both the relative factor proportions used in a given industry and in the choice of industry for expansion. For economies as large and as varied as India, Pakistan and Brazil this seems implausible. The capital and foreign exchange requirements involved in modernising their agricultural sectors bear a very different relationship to the value of output compared with steel mills and heavy electrical and mechanical engineering complexes. Cheap and efficient stationary diesel engines for driving tubewell pumps are being produced in West Pakistan in village workshops by very labour intensive methods. Tubewell strainers in Pakistan are now largely made from fibre ropes wrapped around iron spacers in place of expensive imported brass strainers. In both Pakistan and India the production of refined sugar has become a relatively important industry. In the case of India sugar is now actually exported. In both economies, but particularly in Pakistan the sucrose recovery rate from crushing the cane is the lowest in the world yet the natural conditions for cane growing are good. In Pakistan the same or greater levels of output of refined sugar could have been obtained with a much smaller capital and foreign exchange cost if instead of investing in many new mills with the latest and most expensive machinery a small fraction of these resources had been devoted to improving the quality of the sugar cane and providing farmers with incentives to achieve higher yields of sugar per acre instead of disease ridden stalks of inferior cane.

The same objective can in many cases be achieved in a variety of ways. Even in something as basic to industry as the generation and distribution of electrical power there are several options, each with a different capital and foreign exchange requirement per kilowatt of output; ranging from nuclear reactors and massive hydro-power schemes to mobile diesel or jet-turbine driven generators. Faulty choices, involving too heavy a capital and foreign exchange cost in power generation due to incorrect evaluation of opportunity costs have been a common feature of many LDCs development programmes.[19] Provided that prices which reflect true opportunity costs are allowed to influence the decisions of private businessmen and farmers on the one hand and government planners on the other it seems to me unlikely that the average factor proportions employed in the economy will not alter so as to make most use of the cheapest factors of production provided their cheapness is not offset by excessively low productivity.

The reason why capital and import intensive industries and methods of production have grown in LDCs can in many cases be attributed to the fact that the relevant prices were distorted by subsidies and controls. Where foreign exchange or imports have been licensed and distributed to businessmen at costs which were far below the true opportunity costs it is not surprising that factories have been built which use Western techniques to produce Western type manufactures. Similarly, if government investment decisions have been based on appraisals which used absurdly low interest rates and official (grossly overvalued) exchange rates it is not surprising that projects should be chosen which use intensively the scarce capital and foreign exchange resources of the economy. The aid policies of donor countries have encouraged LDCs to undertake projects which called for capital equipment and current inputs which had to be imported, often under tied aid which raised their costs.[20]

Linder's model assumes only two types of imports and leaves out consumer goods. This is legitimate only if they are already at an irreducible minimum. This might appear plausible given the batteries of controls and high taxation which most LDCs impose upon imports of consumer goods. One might accept that LDCs which are trying hard to speed up development have by now cut consumption imports down to the minimum were it not for the fact that food imports figure so prominently in their balance of payments. Of course a major part of these have been obtained under concessional terms, but both India and Pakistan have been forced into the open market to purchase wheat and rice with their own foreign exchange. Whether sufficient food aid for their needs will be forthcoming in the 1970s is extremely dubious.

The neglect of imports of goods for final consumption also runs a risk of underplaying their importance in economic development. Some may be incentive goods necessary to stimulate farmers and other workers to extra efforts and sacrifices in order to achieve higher real consumption standards. As Stolper put it:

'Farmers are quite aware of the choice of goods that exists. But they have no money illusion, and they need to be assured that an increase in their income as the result of their efforts

can be translated into particular goods with frequently involve
imports: cement houses with tin roofs; transistor radios;
bicycles; motor scooters . . .'[21].

In both countries the terms of trade were deliberately shifted
against agriculture so as to transfer resources to industry.[22] A good
deal of both India's and Pakistan's recent agricultural problems can
be ascribed to these policies. The repercussion from agricultural
weaknesses have been felt on both the import and the export side of
their balance of payments.

It is at least arguable that the major reasons for such countries
recurrent balance of payments difficulties can be ascribed to policies
which violated traditional allocation theory and to faulty expenditure
policies. Industries set up on the basis of infant industry or import
substitution criteria have often proved to be very retarded infants.
They have in many cases failed to cover their costs of operation and
have consequently depended on subsidies with their significant
budgetary implications, or on continued high tariffs or import
controls. These have contributed to inflationary pressures and have
also directly affected costs of producing intermediate products and
thus exports. It is notable that countries considered to be foreign
exchange gap examples do all seem to suffer from fairly rapid
inflation. Taking $1958 = 100$ the cost of living indices were in 1966:

Argentina	958
Brazil	3,010
Chile	583
Colombia	243
India	166
Pakistan	143

Source: IMF *International Financial Statistics* November 1967.

In both India and Pakistan the supply of between 5 and 10 per cent
of their annual food requirements from PL 480 concessional (virtually
free) imports has been an important factor in dampening the inflation which would otherwise have occurred.

Export limit

In a recent article[23] Professor Benjamin Cohen has demonstrated
how import restrictions can have a fairly immediate impact upon
export prices quite apart from the longer run effects due to re-
allocation of productive resources. Even if import duties on raw
materials are refunded to exporters, intermediate goods which they
purchase will reflect changed imported import costs and will raise
the costs of exported manufactures damaging their international
competitiveness. It is also rare for compensation to be given to

producers for the effects of quantitative controls in the prices of imports. For Colombia a 20 per cent increase in certain import prices would raise the cost of Colombian textiles by about 12 per cent.[24]

High levels of protection persisted in for considerable periods of time will also damage export prospects both by shifting resources towards import competing industry and by reducing the stimulus to efficiency which foreign competition can bring.

One of the weaknesses of Linder's approach to the empirical testing of his theories is a tendency to look at the LDCs as a whole while the exchange gap theory may apply only to a limited number of countries. The difficulties which face exporters of primary products in terms of low price elasticities of demand for their exports look far worse when viewed in this way. The price elasticity of demand facing cotton may be substantially less than unity, but for Pakistan's raw cotton and cotton goods the price elasticities are in principle high[25]. If developed countries violate the free trade rules and impose restrictions on imports when demand for Pakistan's cotton goods rises as a result of their relative cheapness then Pakistan's exports may be frustrated but not because of low price elasticity. Linder does acknowledge the point about the higher country elasticity but argues that, 'What is ultimately interesting is the impact on the developing countries in the aggregate. Therefore, it seems reasonable to base estimates of the export maximum on the less elastic demand curve facing the group – all the more so as independent action by one country is likely to lead to retaliation.'[26]

The first statement seems wrong. Governments are responsible for national economic policies and trade theories are intended to give guidance on the formulation of these policies. If several countries suffer from inflation and one succeeds in controlling this the price elasticities facing it are highly relevant. The recent devaluation of the Indian rupee was not followed by either Pakistan or Ceylon, India's closest trade rivals. If, as I and at least some other commentators believe, the true exchange gap situation exists for only a limited number of countries which have demonstrated a reasonably high absorptive capacity for additional foreign exchange resources then it is the market prospects for their exports that matters.

When the market prospects for the present primary product exports of LDCs are examined they seem rather poor. The rate of growth of world demand for many of them is slow and the price elasticities facing them are low. However, if an individual LDC has a substantial cost advantage it may still do very well by increasing its exports of a primary good. Those with oil, certain other minerals and natural gas are faced by relatively buoyant markets and need have few worries over foreign exchange gaps. Others may switch from present primary goods to new primary exports as the changing needs of industry raise demands for minerals and metals whose economic value has not yet been realised. Some may succeed in raising their productivity, lowering their costs and fighting a successful battle against the incursions of synthetics or displacing rival supplies of the natural products. Malaysia, in natural rubber, has certainly fought a very successful rearguard action against synthetics by deploying considerable resources in research to improve the qualities of natural rubber, raise the productivity of the rubber trees and to encourage diversification into palm oil. Other countries may be able to do the same.

The problems of some of the LDCs which have experienced severe balance of payments deficits can be explained in large part by faulty expenditure policies and inefficient allocational policies. In addition to the points made above there are the views of analysts such as A.K.Cairncross and the GATT Report *Trends in International Trade*.[27] They argue that LDCs export difficulties have been due primarily to slow growth in domestic output of traditional exports plus rapid expansion of domestic demand for some of their traditional exports. Support for these views comes from an analysis of India's export problems in a recent article by B.I.Cohen.[28] He argues that India's difficulties stem from a decline in her share of expanding world markets for her traditional exports, that this was caused by a rise in the relative prices of Indian goods and that these price increases were the result of India's policies which were inconsistent with giving a high priority to export promotion. Analyses of statistics on 16 major Indian exports and analyses of Indian economic policies in this article give good grounds for accepting his view that during the First and Second Indian Five Year Plans policies followed by the Indian government were the principal cause of India's poor export performance.[29]

Some commentators would be prepared to argue that policies of import substitution and excessively rapid industrialisation have damaged the export potential of several of the most important Latin American countries.

There is a good deal of evidence which suggests that the balance of payments difficulties of these LDCs which appear to fit the exchange gap analysis stem from inept expenditure policies, incorrect exchange rates and faulty use of prices in allocating resources. Of course this is concerned with causes, not effects. A country which has got itself into difficulties through past policy errors may nevertheless have an excellent case for aid to pay for current input imports as well as for investment resources. The *de facto* situation in India, at least, is one where its economic growth is constrained at least for some time by shortage of imports rather than inability to increase domestic savings. The shadow price for foreign exchange then becomes very high and policies to conserve foreign exchange for current inputs are justified, but this does not imply the blank cheque for import substitution which Linder advocates as a main policy conclusion of his analysis.

Linder's criteria for import substitution

His recommendation is that a country with an actual or potential exchange gap should substitute domestic production for imports whenever this gives a net saving in foreign exchange, i.e. the value of the imports replaced during the life of the investment must exceed the imports, both capital and current inputs, required for the project. [30] This is a very easy criterion and one that could often conflict with normal allocation criteria. The assumption underpinning this criterion is that the marginal cost of employing domestic factors of production is zero. This is supposed to follow from the fact that the import bottleneck would otherwise have prevented their employment at all. Any saving on imports allows capacity to be employed which would otherwise stand idle.

One cannot know whether a given project will overall produce a net saving in foreign exchange until one has gone through an elaborate input-output analysis and even then any conclusion is subject to the usual assumptions of constant coefficients and no alterations in prices. In addition to the direct import cost of the production of the import substitutes there are the repercussions on other domestic industries and in turn on their imports and exports. Net imports may increase. Even on its own assumptions of the existence of a genuine exchange gap. Linder's criterion is too narrow.

The criterion also assumes implicitly that the foreign exchange gap will continue throughout the lifetime of the project. This could of course be a self-justifying prophecy given the results which would probably stem from a policy of indiscriminate import substitution. But if in a few years the gap would in any case have ceased to be a constraint so that the economy would not be prevented by lack of exchange from achieving full capacity operation, other criteria become important, e.g. the rate of return on the investment after allowing for externalities.

Each new project will make demands on a number of inputs. Some of these, not only foreign exchange, will be in scarce supply. Management, including foremen, and skilled workers are particularly scarce in many LDCs. The new project may have to bid them away from other activities. This cost to the economy should be measured in any

24   A.I.MACBEAN

evaluation of a new investment, but is ignored by the Linder criterion. This could only be legitimate if such factors of production were in excess supply owing to the under utilization of present capacity. However, it is not the common experience that industries are willing to release experienced management and skilled labour in these situations; rather will they treat them as fixed overheads.

A project which produces a net saving in foreign exchange but does not earn over its lifetime a normal return on capital will require to be subsidised or protected by government. This will impose fiscal burdens on the government and possibly damage incentives to work, save and invest. If the subsidies are not covered by taxation there will be risks of inflation and further distortion in the allocation of resources. Either tax increases or increased protection will reduce the standard of living of the citizens of the country: scarcely a legitimate objective of development policy.

A net saving on foreign exchange is an inadequate criterion for planning purposes. Too many other scarce factors are involved and investment criteria must take account of their scarcity. This means that projects must be analysed on the basis of all their costs and benefits. Where necessary, adjustments to the accounting prices used should be made to take account of relative scarcities which are not reflected in the prices which have to be paid. External economies and diseconomies where quantifiable should be included in the analysis. Where the official rate of exchange does not reflect the true scarcity of foreign currency a shadow rate of exchange should be used in the evaluation. The very difficult task of estimating plausible magnitudes for this rate represents one important foreign trade aspect of development planning.

Acknowledgments

I am indebted to Rowland Maddock and Tin Nguyen of the University of Lancaster for comments on a draft of this paper and to the members of Edinburgh International Economics Seminar for comments made in discussion of the paper there.

Notes and references

1 UN *Commodity Trade and Economic Development* (1953) p. 10 H. Singer 'The Distribution of Gains Between Investing and Borrowing Countries' *Am. Econ. Review* (May 1950) 473.
 B. Higgins Economic Development (1959) p. 155.
2 A. MacBean *Export Instability and Economic Development* (1966).
3 A. MacBean *op cit.* p. 58.
4 S. Kuznets *Six Lectures on Economic Growth* (1959) pp. 89–107.
5 M. Michaely *Concentration in International Trade* (1962) Table 17.
6 A. MacBean *op cit.* pp. 60–61.
7 UN Document No. 55, II, G.2 (New York 1955) and UN *Towards a New Trade Policy for Development* (New York 1964).

8 H.B. Chenery and M. Bruno 'Development Alternatives in an Open Economy: The case of Israel' *Econ. Journal* (March 1962).
Chenery and Strout 'Foreign Assistance and Economic Development' *Am. Econ. Review* (Sept. 1966).
J. Vanek *Estimating Foreign Resource Needs for Economic Development* (1967).

9 R. McKinnon 'Foreign Exchange Constraints in Economic Development and Efficient Aid Allocation' *Econ. Journal* (June 1964).
A. MacBean *op cit.* pp. 111–2. A mimeographed paper by David Wall 'Imports, Import Capacity and Economic Growth' (Feb. 1967) makes similar points.

10 Wall *op. cit.*

11 Internal subsidies and taxes are in any case likely to be a more efficient method of correcting existing price distortions than tariffs.

12 S.B. Linder *Trade and Trade Policy for Development* (London 1967).

13 Linder *op. cit.* p. 36.

14 Linder *An Essay on Trade Transformation* (New York 1961) pp. 82–109.

15 Linder *Trade and Trade Policy for Development* (London 1967) p. 37.

16 A report by the Swedish Importers' and Wholesalers' Organization, March 12, 1963, quoted in Linder *Trade and Trade Policy for Development* p. 37.

17 Linder *op. cit.* p. 50.

18 C.F. I.M.D. Little *Aid to Africa* (Oxford 1964) and R. Dumont *False Start in Africa.*

19 Cf. Neil Jacoby *An Evaluation of U.S. Economic Aid to Free China 1951– 1965*, A.I.D. Discussion Paper No. 11, 1966, p. 89.

20 Mahbub ul Haq 'Tied Credits. A Quantitative Analysis', Paper given to the Round Table Conference on Capital Movements and Economic Development, Washington, July, 1965.

21 W. Stolper *Planning Without Facts* (Cambridge, Mass. 1966) p. 142.

22 Cf. G. Papaneck *Pakistan's Economic Development* (Cambridge, Mass. 1967).

23 B.I. Cohen 'Measuring the Short-Run Impact of a Country's Import Restrictions on its Exports' *The Quarterly Journal of Economics* (August 1966).

24 Cohen *op. cit.* Table 1 pp. 460–1.

25 The formula for calculating the price elasticity facing one country is

$$E = \frac{E_w + KS_w}{1 - K} \text{ where}$$

E is the country's export demand elasticity,
E_w is the elasticity of demand facing the product in world markets.
K is the share of the market taken by the rest of the world
S_w is the price elasticity of supply of the rest of the world
If $E_w = 0.6$, $K = 0.8$, $S_w = 0.5$ then $E = 5.0$

26 Linder *op. cit.* p. 40.

27 'International Trade and Economic Development', Kyklos, XIII (1960)
GATT *Trends in International Trade, A report by a Panel of Experts* (Geneva 1958).

28 'The Stagnation of Indian Exports, 1951–61' *Quarterly Journal of Economics* (Nov. 1964) (based on his Harvard, Ph.D. thesis).

29 Cohen *op. cit.* pp. 606–17.

30 Linder *op cit.* pp. 90–2.

PETER ADY

International Commodity Policy

The commodity problem has been a feature of the international scene for about a half century. Between the wars commodity price fluctuations were severe. They were also roughly synchronised with a phasing which coincided with that of the trade cycle. An early UN report[1] says:

'A conspicuous feature of commodity price movements during the first half of the twentieth century was the magnitude of cyclical variations. While the year-to-year fluctuations in prices were large in themselves, the degree of instability was heightened by the fact that prices tended to move in the same direction for several successive years. *For this reason, measurement of year-to-year fluctuations alone understates the degree of instability.* Although the timing, duration and amplitude of cyclical movements varied from commodity to commodity, there was a strong tendency for prices to fluctuate together'.

After the war it was widely expected that commodity price fluctuation would be much mitigated and perhaps even disappear with full employment. And this has, to some extent, proved to be the case. The UN report quoted above argued that swings became more violent after the second world war, but the immediate post-war years were hardly typical. They include (i) the abolition of international price control in 1947; (ii) general devaluation against the dollar in 1949; and (iii) the Korean War inflation of 1950–1.

Fluctuations have in fact declined in the fifties and sixties with full employment. This can be seen from table 1 which covers a period of 16 years after the devaluations of 1949. But the commodity problem has continued to be spoken of as one of instability. Before we can begin to consider solutions we must ask just what the problem is. Is there a problem of instability which is peculiar to commodities? If so, is the unsatisfactory aspect of commodity markets a matter of price instability or of fluctuations in proceeds? Does the problem face all primary producers or is it peculiar to developing countries, who constantly complain that their growth is held back by fluctuations in their export income?

We will begin therefore with a brief analysis of the commodity problem in general. Section II will deal with the developing countries' problem in commodity exports, for these goods still constitute 85

TABLE 1　Export price indices for primary commodities (1958=100)

Primary exports by	1952	1953	1954	1955	1956	1957	1958	1959	1960	1961	1962	1963	1964	1965	1966	1967
Developed countries	112	108	105	103	105	106	100	99	99	100	99	103	107	108	110	107
Developing countries	106	101	105	103	102	105	100	95	94	90	89	93	95	94	94	93

Source: UN Monthly Bulletin of Statistics for March of each year. Special Tables.

per cent of their export earnings. Section III will touch upon the problem of aid versus trade, while in section IV we shall turn to consider commodity agreements as a possible solution (for others are often canvassed). In this final section, time will not permit a detailed description of agreements and those under discussion, but questions of detail can be settled only by reference to agreement texts and by historical analysis too full to be undertaken here.

I. INSTABILITY OR TREND

The paper begins with some evidence to suggest that instability is today less acute a problem than it was between the wars. In saying this however I should add that I do not mean to endorse the results of two recent statistical studies on this question: one by Professor J. D. Coppock[2] and the other by Professor Alastair MacBean.[3] These are weighty studies, both recently published, and I must turn aside for a moment to say why I do not find them convincing. Both these writers have developed a measure of year-to-year changes which is then used to test, by multivariate analysis, for the influence of instability, as defined, upon the nature of the economic problems of the developing countries. Using time series for 1946–58 (Coppock) or 1946–59 (MacBean) these two investigators have reported that instability is no worse in world primary product markets than in 'world markets' for manufactures. This particular comparison rests upon Professor Coppock's analysis but it is endorsed by Alastair MacBean who quotes Coppock's findings.

Professor Coppock has developed a measure of instability,[4] and has applied this to his published data for 83 countries. He finds that instability is not specially peculiar to commodity markets, nor is it highly correlated with the problems of the developing countries. I have some difficulty in accepting his results, however, since they seem to me much affected by the particular period selected for study. Unfortunately Professor Coppock has fallen into the trap of using a broken series to measure instability. The break comes in 1949 with world-wide devaluation against the dollar. It is a break which differently affected each country, as will easily be appreciated. Worse still it also differently affects reported world values for each commodity.

This latter criticism can most easily be illustrated by reference to Professor Coppock's most often quoted result, 'Contrary to widely held views, *export proceeds were decidedly more stable for primary goods than for manufactured goods*'. (p. 35). We can see where he gets this impression if we consider what happened to prices on devaluation (table 2).

Now Coppock has used dollar values throughout his study. In

TABLE 2 Export unit values indices in world trade (1950=100)

	Manufactures		Primary products	
	$	£	$	£
1948	119	83	104	72
1949	114	85	96	72
1950	100		100	
1951	122		126	

Source: UN Monthly Bulletin of Statistics, March 1954, Special Table A.

dollar terms the prices of manufactures fluctuated far more violently than did those of primary products, for the USA was the main importer of the manufactures of the other developed countries in this period, all of which had devalued. The situation was different in primary products: the UK and Western Europe were important markets for many foodstuffs and raw materials and most of their supplies came from countries which also devalued with them. If we look at figure 1 we can see just how different the picture would be if 1949 were omitted from the calculations by starting the series in 1950 or later. [5]

If we add to the destabilising effect of devaluation upon prices its impact upon the volume of exports of manufactures, we find a second reason why export *proceeds* fluctuated more for manufactures than for primary goods, exportable supplies of which were less elastic in the first post-war decade.

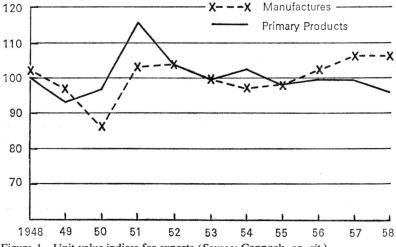

Figure 1 Unit value indices for exports (*Source:* Coppock, *op. cit.*)

Professor Coppock's general statements about commodities also raise some doubts, for the global commodity figures are no better. Aggregation conceals changes through off-setting effects as Professor Coppock's own figures show, e.g. compare his estimate of price instability in primary products[6] as a whole (8.4) with the weighted average value obtained (20.4, with a range of 7 to 41) when done on a commodity-by-commodity basis.[7] Coppock himself observes of this result in a footnote on the same page, 'Interestingly, these are close to the typical figures for the 83 countries'. (See figure 2.) But Coppock leaves the matter there; and so perhaps should we,

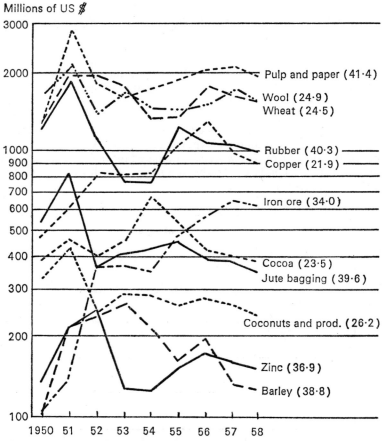

Figure 2   Value of selected world exports, 1950–8 (*Source:* Coppock, *op. cit.*)

with reflections on misplaced aggregation, as Professor Streeten terms it.

Professor MacBean also subscribes to the view that instability is not a problem for primary producers and if we define it and them as he does, we should I think agree with him (except where he quotes Professor Coppock, which he does somewhat too frequently). Professor MacBean's definition of instability is narrower, however, than many realise, for he measures instability as deviations from a five-year moving average. He does not publish charts or tables of his moving average, but knowledge of the period suggests that his method of removing trend may also remove cyclical swings. This phenomenon is well known. In a series which itself shows instability of a period longer than the five years this measure would understate any residual instability involved. While the US trade cycle since 1946 may have a four-year periodicity, the cycle in commodity prices[8] still seems to run at eight to ten years (see table 3).

If this view is correct, then given his rather restricted definition of instability it is not surprising that Professor MacBean finds it to play so small a part in explaining the trade and development difficulties of the developing countries. As to the influence of instability upon economic growth, MacBean says, 'All in all, our search for evidence demonstrating the adverse influence of short-term instability of export earnings on the prospects of growth in underdeveloped countries gives us no grounds for believing that export instability is in fact so harmful'. (p. 127.)

These nil results are still less surprising when we remember other features of the period he perforce investigated, for this period is riddled with factors extraneous to the sort of hypotheses he is testing. These factors include the influence of devaluation, the Korean War, the dollar shortage till 1957 and consequent trade ties. This is also a period before planning had really accelerated economic growth in the developing countries and before foreign exchange had become the bottleneck to their growth which it now is.[9]

Finally I must put the point that it is again misplaced aggregation (found in both Coppock and MacBean) to treat primary products as a homogeneous class. Not only must we look separately at temperate and tropical products, but we must distinguish between agricultural and mineral products. There are difficulties about interpreting statements which relate to primary products as a whole, when conditions are so different in different sectors. In many commodities production is so organised that the adjustment of supply to changing demand conditions is fairly flexible, e.g. minerals, oil and many temperate crops. Since the last war the speed of adjustment in these favoured commodities has been increased by government

TABLE 3   Price index of primary commodities in world trade (1958=100)

		Food			Agricultural non-food		Textiles		Minerals	
			of which							
	Total	Total	Coffee tea, cocoa	Cereals	Total	Fats, oils, oil seeds	Total	of which Wool	Total	of which Metal ores
1950	101	97	93	109	122	106	151	170	83	83
1951	124	109	103	124	168	134	204	223	96	108
1952	110	107	101	126	123	111	137	129	100	115
1953	104	106	106	122	111	106	128	145	93	100
1954	109	114	145	112	113	111	133	137	94	94
1955	104	102	109	105	115	101	125	125	95	98
1956	–105–	–101–	–106–	–102–	–114–	–109–	–123–	–129–	–99–	–105–
1957	106	103	103	100	113	105	126	144	103	107
1958	100	100	100	100	100	100	100	100	100	100
1959	97	93	83	97	105	100	98	106	94	97
1960	97	91	77	96	107	94	104	108	93	98
1961	95	90	72	98	103	97	105	107	92	100
1962	94	90	70	103	99	89	101	106	92	99
1963	100	103	73	102	103	95	112	127	92	96
1964	103	106	87	105	105	98	116	131	94	104
1965	100	99	80	101	104	108	105	110	96	110
1966	101	100	84	107	105	105	106	115	97	110

Linked at 1953 in shifting earlier year to time base at 1958.

– – UN series linked at 1956. For details of weighting, etc., see p. xv November 1953.

Source: UN Monthly Bulletin of Statistics Special Table A (Quarterly).

interventions in the richer countries. These include holding stocks off the market (e.g. the North American Wheat Boards, the US Commodity Credit Corporation) and subsidising of farmers either to increase production or even to decrease it (e.g. the US Soil Bank Scheme). The capacity of the developing countries to adjust commodity supply to changing demand or to moderate productivity gains is limited, if not totally lacking, especially in agriculture.

Basically the Coppock/MacBean approach does not seem to illuminate the real issues in commodity problems. The measure of short-run instability[10] which each has used perhaps does indicate the nature and frequency of temporary difficulties, but it is hard to believe that the developing countries would make such heavy weather of such transient phenomena. Between the wars the problems arose from long cyclical swings. The post-war world has seen a decade of high prices and another of low prices. Is this a cycle ? Or does the present low level portend a trend ? Is Prebisch right in saying that there is a declining *trend* and that this may be expected to continue ?

II. THE TERMS OF TRADE

It is of course fashionable to say that there is no trend: that the terms of trade of primary producers today are exactly what they were in 1937, in 1928, in 1913. But the terms of trade is a peculiar statistic. In its simplest form, the commodity terms of trade compares weighted average of prices of goods exported by countries with those imported. Over long periods the composition of the bundle of commodity exports and of imports both change, and problems of interpretation arise.

We are on safer ground examining export prices and import prices separately. It becomes immediately obvious that we would not expect export prices to decline, decade after decade, i.e. in the long period, because supply adjustments would take place. The question can then be analysed into two parts: (i) What is happening to demand for primary products ? (ii) What is the period of supply adjustment ? Since 1945 there have been changes on the demand side which have adversely affected the competitive position of most tropical agricultural exports, a full account of which is to be found in the GATT Report,[11] Nurkse[12] and Maizels.[13] The main features of these changes can be summed up on the demand side as increasing self-sufficiency in importing countries, through technical progress and the growth of synthetics. On the supply side, tropical countries appear to be on the threshold of technical improvements in agriculture which are likely to increase the embarrassment of surpluses.

When the primary product exports of the developed countries are aggregated separately from those of the developing countries the different time paths of the export prices of each since 1956 is striking. The decline in prices facing the developing countries is the essence of the commodity problem.

The disturbing feature of this picture is that tropical countries are the least able to bring about rapid supply adjustments because of their underdeveloped character, and the lack of alternative livelihood for their labour. There has thus been a big change in the commodity problem since 1945, which means that we can no longer consider the traditional exports of the LDCs in the same terms as those of the industrialised countries.

We do not need to appeal to statistics therefore to forecast a declining trend of prices for most tropical products. But, as it so happens, the post-war statistics also indicate a falling tendency in export prices and in the terms of trade of tropical primary products against manufactures whether we take 1950–1, 1953–4 or 1956–7 as our starting point. This tendency can be separately identified in each commodity group (see table 3).

The terms of trade effect

It may still be argued that these factors do not constitute a problem since the developing countries can maintain their export earnings in the face of falling prices by increasing the volume sold abroad. By this reckoning falling prices do not matter so long as proceeds remain more or less stable. This argument, of course, assumes high price elasticity of demand, which does not obtain for tropical foodstuffs. Where demand elasticity is high, as in the natural raw materials, it can be argued moreover that a fall in export prices represents a resource loss to the exporting country, even if increased volumes sold do succeed in maintaining earnings. This is a period of history in which the developed countries have proclaimed that they do not wish to gain resources at the expense of the developing world. Indeed their expressed intention is that transfers should go the other way. The magnitude of the transfer involved through falling export prices can be estimated by applying Geary's measure of trading gains and losses obtained in the deflating of national accounts.

If we begin with accounts in current prices

$$Y = C + I + X - M.$$

These flows can all be deflated by appropriate prices indices to give

$$Y' = C' + I' + X' - M'.$$

Now we may find that whereas $X - M$ is positive $X' - M'$ is negative, or *vice versa*. What is more, we would find that if we deflate N the foreign balance independently, its deflated value would not be the same as $(X'-M')$, whatever the deflator we use for N. To make the two sides again equal we must add T' such that

$$I' = N' - (X' - M')$$

where T' = the trading loss or gain through prices,

i.e. $T' = -\left(\dfrac{X}{P_x} - \dfrac{M}{P_m}\right) + N'.$

There are problems as to which price index to use to deflate N', since this is not a flow,[14] but the strongest candidates are the import price index or export price index. The upshot is much the same in either case.

If we divide N by P_x this gives

$$T' = -\left(\frac{X}{P_x} - \frac{M}{P_m}\right) + \frac{X-M}{P_x} = -M\left(\frac{1}{P_x} - \frac{1}{P_m}\right).$$

If we divide N by P_m this gives

$$T' = -\left(\frac{X}{P_x} - \frac{M}{P_m}\right) + \frac{X-M}{P_m} = -X\left(\frac{1}{P_x} - \frac{1}{P_m}\right).$$

The only difference between these formulae is that you apply it to the import bill at current prices in the first case and to exports in the second.

If we apply this formula to the developing countries as a whole we can estimate the resource loss through the terms of trade effect as between 1958 and 1966.[15] While exports of all kinds from the developing world to developed countries had fallen to an index of 98 by 1966 (1958 = 100) the unit value of their imports from developed countries had risen to 105 on the same base year. Total exports and imports of the developing world were $35·7 billion and $37·4 billion respectively. Whence multiplying by exports we have,

$$T' = -\$b\ 35·7\ (\tfrac{1}{98} - \tfrac{1}{105}) = -\$b\ 2·49.$$

The terms of trade of the developing countries have fallen only five points since 1958 (see table 4) and the unit value of their exports as a whole has fallen by two points. These changes may seem small but remember that this is a highly aggregated index: it includes oil whose prices are administered prices and metals and minerals whose market values have been inflated by the war in Vietnam. Yet the great majority of developing countries export neither oil nor minerals and their own terms of trade look very different. Also included in this seemingly stable series are the many countries whose exports consist largely of traditional crops, in which prices have been falling

TABLE 4 Terms of trade and unit value indices of exports and imports (1958=100)

	1952	1953	1954	1955	1956	1957	1958	1959	1960	1961	1962	1963	1964	1965	1966
Trade with rest of world															
Developed areas	98	99	97	97	98	99	100	101	101	102	102	102	101	102	102
Underdeveloped areas	106	104	109	109	106	103	100	98	97	95	93	95	96	95	95
Trade between developed and underdeveloped areas															
1. Terms of trade	108	105	112	110	108	103	100	97	96	93	91	93	95	93	93
2. Export price index of under-developed areas	—	—	—	105	105	104	100	97	98	95	92	95	97	98	98
3. Import price index of under-developed areas	—	—	—	95	97	101	100	100	101	102	101	102	103	104	105

Source: UN Monthly Bulletin of Statistics, November 1968, Special Table C, Sub-tables IV and II.

since 1958 or thereabouts. We must also remember that many LDCs are highly specialised in one or two commodities, e.g. Ghana in cocoa, Mauritius in sugar. A small change in aggregate terms of trade may disguise a severe effect for an individual country.

The scale of this resource transfer and current pessimism as to the trade prospects of the LDCs' traditional exports is the mainspring of UNCTAD's efforts to promote acceptance of an international policy for LDCs' commodity exports. LDCs cannot base their plea for international agreements upon natural justice; for there is, of course, no greater validity about one level of prices rather than another or indeed about one distribution of resources (or income) rather than another. However, given the developed world's expressed wish to assist the developing countries, an unplanned resource loss of this magnitude is naturally viewed with some concern. With pessimistic forecasts of further decline the question then arises: should this continued drain on resources be prevented by commodity agreements or should it be offset by compensatory aid ?

III. AID VERSUS TRADE

Arguments in favour of aid rather than commodity price support concentrate upon the desirability of allowing a free play of market forces in world markets. They stress the danger that interference through agreements may make commodity market situations worse by increasing supplies of goods already in surplus, if they result in higher prices. It is pointed out that it is better for countries to shift resources now into new uses rather than to hang on in old lines of activity, producing goods the world no longer wants. Far better to let commodity prices find their own level, so the argument goes, and to give the developing countries more aid instead, to direct resources into new forms of employment.

No simple *laissez-faire* prescription will do. To hope that falling prices alone will drive factors into other uses contains serious fallacies. Either it rests upon the concealed assumption that other means of livelihood are readily available to the peasant producers of export crops and thus fails to recognise certain basic features of underdevelopment; or it fails to recognise the loss of resources consequent upon a price decline. Development economists now generally concede that many, if not most peasant export crops are in actual or theoretical surplus so that no alternatives offer easily in agricultural exports; and that in agricultural production for the home market, alternative opportunities for cash earnings are limited by a scarcity of capital required both by individuals (dairy herds requiring milking equipment, refrigeration etc.) and by the agricultural community (roads, canning factories, water supplies etc.). They also recognise

that the need for complementary inputs is greater still, if labour is to
be moved out of the surplus crop and out of agriculture altogether:
capital costs per new workplace in non-agricultural employment are
high even in developing countries[16] (not less than $3000 per man
and usually more like $10,000). Finally, there is the financing
problem: resources to increase capital formation, whether in domestic agriculture or outside it, are not as readily accumulated by a small
country when its commodity export prices are falling as when they
are rising, given that equipment has to be bought abroad.

Thus the *laissez-faire* prescription fails to recognise the loss of resources which is the consequence of falling export prices whatever
the volumes of trade. It does not explain how such an industry can
itself find the resources to transfer factors to other pursuits, nor
indeed how the government could provide the transfer capital needed
when world prices for a major export are falling, i.e., how such an
industry can be taxed, when its prices are falling, to promote a
transfer into other sectors of the economy.

If falling commodity prices were fully compensated for by increased aid these difficulties would disappear. But this element in
aid flows would then become different in its rationale from existing
flows. It would have to be distributed in a geographical pattern
corresponding to trade losses; and it would have to be geared in
some way to commodity price changes, if long delays were not to
ensue. Finally, it would have to be automatically forthcoming, if
political and other considerations[17] were not to affect its distribution
between countries suffering the price decline. If aid were to be provided in a fully compensatory and automatic way it would be in
effect no different from a well-designed commodity agreement.

In fact compensatory aid of this kind is unlikely to be forthcoming
to judge by past experience. Even if some donor countries recognised
such needs, acceptance of compensatory transfers might well be
denied by others. The developing countries would then get only
partial compensation for their resource losses. In the present climate
of world opinion on aid, it is only too likely that compensatory
transfers, where accepted, would substitute for other transfers to
developing countries so that the net resource transfer might not be
any higher than it is now.[18] As things stand there are a number of
developing countries where trade losses more than offset even the
nominal value of aid.

One proposal half way between aid and a general commodity
agreement has been under negotiation since UNCTAD I, called
Supplementary Financing. This would guarantee countries against
any unforeseen declines in their *export proceeds*. This scheme would
be of assistance in some situation but it does not operate against a

resource drain through *expected* declines in prices nor against an unforeseen price fall if this is offset by a rise in volume. This scheme does not, therefore, compensate for losses through the terms of trade.

One of the arguments for the traditional variety of commodity agreements is that they can be designed to prevent an unwitting further transfer of resources from developing countries by a fully automatic mechanism in which all importing countries must willy-nilly participate.[19] In their most up-to-date variant they can also be designed to separate the maintained world price from that paid to producers. A two-tier price system is now a familiar weapon in agricultural policy: in rich countries the farmers' price is often higher than that paid by the market consumer; in poor countries the producer price is often lower. Since the great peasant export crop economies of Africa and Asia already run dual pricing systems, while Latin America pursues such tax objectives through multiple exchange rates, the stage is already set in most developing countries for this modern version of commodity agreement.

This separation of the distributive from the allocative function of prices means that agreements need not result in increased surpluses. Some economists would go further, quoting experience in developed as well as developing countries that, within a framework of guaranteed prices, producers react more swiftly to incentives to change.

IV. COMMODITY AGREEMENTS

The argument so far has been that the most important aspect of commodity problems in developing countries is that of structural adjustment and that properly designed commodity agreements are a good way, some would say the only way, of bringing about the structural changes needed in developing countries.

International commodity agreements can be used for the promotion of increasing productivity by introduction of taxes to direct a part of the resources procured by the Agreement into channels which promote greater efficiency and, if necessary, diversification into other output. For example, the Coffee Agreement is trying rather belatedly to create a Diversification Fund by voluntary agreement between signatories. Some such levy system should be made conditional by consumer countries, before they next agree to ratify a new scheme. How widespread is this need and which countries and which commodity markets would benefit ?

The brief answer is that every developing country (except Hong-kong, Aden and Singapore) exports some primary commodity. However, only 60 per cent of all commodity exports (including minerals and metals) fall in the category which requires price support and which could benefit from 'organisation of markets' as the French term it. If we exclude minerals and metals from the commodity total on the score that marketing of such commodities is already well organised, the proportion rises to over 70 per cent (see table 5). But not all commodities allow of a simple type arrangement and we shall have to consider commodities under two headings.

Commodities suitable for traditional types of agreement. As we can see from the classification given in table 5 only the commodities listed in category 1a are suitable for the traditional variety of agreement which maintains price by limiting the supply to the market. These commodities constitute 26 per cent of developing countries' exports of primary products of all kinds, which is a sizeable fraction of exports. They are also widely produced in developing countries. Agreements already exist for coffee and tin: if they could be introduced for the others which are all agricultural items,[20] it would benefit a great many countries. Yet of these three other crops an agreement for cocoa is the only one under discussion.[21] Tea prices are only now beginning to slide, and an agreement has been suggested by Ceylon, but opposed by India. There are special reasons why a bananas agreement is not being canvassed.

Other commodity exports of the developing countries. Schemes for the other agricultural exports of the developing countries are more difficult to organise multilaterally, because of competition from close substitutes, which make traditional methods of supply restriction ineffective. Nevertheless other methods of market organisation are available as to whose usefulness there is now a widespread consensus of international opinion[22] and whose practicability has been demonstrated in experiments such as the minimum import price schemes for sugar;[23] for wheat and butter (operated by the UK); and for tropical oils and oilseeds (by France). Under the International Wheat Agreement a new ingredient is the internationally financed Food Aid element, by which consuming countries pay their share across the exchanges for the transfer of up to 5 million tons of wheat a year to the World Food Programme. The International Wheat Agreement, with its minimum import price and quota provisions and its Surplus Disposal provisions in the Food Aid element, shows that such schemes are practicable once the major consumers accept their obligations. If the price of wheat imports under the IWA can be kept £2 a ton higher by such means, when the main exporting beneficiaries are the world's richest countries, there seems no special idealism about suggesting that similar arrangements be applied elsewhere.

TABLE 5   A classification of commodities[1] exported by developing countries, according to the existence or otherwise of substitutes in consumption and trade barriers

	Principal commodities[2]	Exports from developing countries 1963–5 average	
		$000 million	per cent
1. *Commodities produced wholly or mainly in developing countries:*			
(a) Not facing serious competition from substitutes (Group I)	Coffee, tea, cocoa, tin, bananas, spices	4·2	*26*
(b) Facing serious competition from substitutes (Group II)	Raw cotton,[3] natural rubber, raw wool,[3] hard fibres, hides and skins,[3] raw jute	3·3	*20*
2. *Commodities produced in substantial amounts in both developed and developing countries:*			
(a) Not facing appreciable trade barriers (Group III)	Copper, iron ore, fish and fishmeal, bauxite, lead, zinc, manganese ore	2·9	*18*
(b) Facing appreciable trade barriers (Group IV)	Sugar, vegetable oils and oilseeds,[3] cereals (including rice), wood, tobacco, wine, citrus fruit, dried fruit and nuts, furskins	5·1	*32*
3. *Commodities produced wholly or mainly in developed countries* (Group V)	Meat (including live animals and canned meat), dairy products (including eggs)	0·7	*4*
Total of above		16·2	*100*

[1] Excluding petroleum.

[2] Within each group, commodities are listed in order of importance, by value, in the total exports of developing countries in 1963–5.

[3] Cotton, wool, hides and skins, and vegetable oils and oilseeds are also produced in substantial amounts in developed countries.

Commodities which would benefit from market organisation include Group 1(a) and 1(b) plus sugar (1085) and vegetable oils and oilseeds (763).

Source: Trade Yearbook, 1966, FAO, Rome, 1967; national statistics.

International schemes for these other commodities are thus practicable, though adaptions of existing patterns may be better still for individual commodity cases. Although the design of each scheme would be better if made upon a commodity-by-commodity basis, this should not be taken to imply that there are commodities for which some form of price support cannot be devised. Despite the high substitution elasticities in these other commodity groups (which make supply restriction ineffective) it is now generally recognised that means can be found to achieve the same ends by a suitable 'organisation of markets', to use the French phrase. For example, another solution to the world sugar problem would be to extend the Food Aid arrangements developed for the International Wheat Agreement, in 1967, to surplus sugar buying. As with wheat, surplus cane-sugar, whose export markets have been frustrated by self-sufficiency programmes in developed countries, could be bought for the World Food Programme at guaranteed prices. This sugar could either be given free to the Third World or sold there at free market prices. The rationale of such solution rests upon:

(i) Compensation by developed countries for damage done to cane-sugar markets by subsidised beet-sugar production.

(ii) A need for sugar, which is highly calorific, in a world of food shortages.

(iii) The fact that sugar is produced in almost every less-developed country so that the benefits of such a scheme would be widespread.

(iv) The fact that developed countries would also benefit since they would export more to the now richer sugar countries.

With productivity still rising in beet production in temperate zone countries, the danger is that existing market support arrangements may be dismantled. It is not an overstatement to say that this threatens catastrophe in many small sugar based economies, like Jamaica and Mauritius. Nor is it an exaggeration to say that the damage to the export potential of such countries will handicap their development. It will also reciprocally reduce the rate of growth of developed countries trade, but unfortunately for the cane-sugar exporters by too small an amount to be noticed.

Design of commodity schemes

The Havana Charter of 1944 is initially responsible for the relative success of commodity schemes now operating. For it enjoins consumer country participation and support. Consumers countries are equally represented nowadays on agreement councils and all important decisions are taken by a distributed majority.

A further influence has been the growing recognition by the industrial countries of the importance to the developing world of a prosperous agriculture. This recognition is partly due to post-war agricultural support policies in the developed countries' own domestic agriculture, and its success in promoting increasing agricultural productivity at home, and partly to an extension of the same principles to developing countries. Since the transformation of agricultural structure needs resources the developed world has shown itself willing to support agreements, even to the extent of policing them, e.g. by the introduction of Certificates of Origin for coffee imports.

There is today also a keener appreciation by the industrial countries of the principles of development economics and of the developing countries' needs and possibilities; for developing countries relying on certain exports are particularly helpless in the face of factors such as subsidised production (e.g. beet sugar) and captive markets (e.g. synthetic raw materials manufactured by their own industrial users). They can compete through lower prices but only at the cost of a continuing loss of real resources,[24] and possibly even without maintaining their export receipts, if volumes do not rise sufficiently to compensate for the price fall, as has just happened with natural rubber. This makes their task of transformation all the more difficult to finance.

Many developed countries[25] are today willing to take part in international commodity arrangements designed to prevent the by now foreseeable transfer to themselves of developing countries' resources through the terms of trade effect. But more would come out in favour if the design of future schemes were to ensure that some part of the resources retained were going to be channelled into the ends of diversification and increased efficiency in the agricultural sector rather than just being passed on to the producers. For one valid objection to price support is the consequent danger of drawing more labour into a possibly non-competitive industry.

This last objection is less important in the many developing countries which are already taxing their commodity export sectors to the limit: the Marketing Boards of ex-British Africa and the francophone counterpart devices;[26] and the multiple exchange rate systems of Latin America. Another safeguard has been devised in proposals for a Diversification Levy on coffee exported under quotas allocated by the International Coffee Agreement.

A fund to provide resources for technical research into the natural product, to improve productivity, on the one hand, and on the other, to find new uses and markets for it is another need. Research is also needed into methods of producing improved varieties of raw material whether at the growing or the processing stage. It is unfortunate that proposals for such a Fund, put forward by the developing countries at the last UNCTAD were not agreed by the developed countries, in the course of the discussions[27] on Synthetics and Substitutes. The developing countries had in mind that some contribution to such research should come from the developed countries and it is clear that without such a contribution the developing countries' research efforts would be paltry in size as compared with that already mounted on synthetics and substitutes, the annual *budget* of which has been put at $1000m. As table 5 shows the annual *outturn* of natural raw materials threatened by this research is no more than $3500m. While no one would wish to argue that technical progress should be slowed down or stopped, some diversion of these research efforts, without a fall in the total, from the synthetics industries to natural raw materials could benefit consumers as much and the developing countries more.

Summing up

This essay began with some evidence to show that instability is more of a problem in commodity export markets than those for manufactures, even though the degree of such instability appears to be smaller than it was between the wars when such severe cycles in demand were experienced. It also draws attention to results by Maizels controverting the Coppock/MacBean findings and supporting the developing countries' view that this short-run instability adversely affects their growth.

The longer period changes in commodity export prices (all downwards in the last ten years), next considered, were shown to have a considerable impact through the terms of trade effect upon the resources available for development. The annual depletion of developing countries' resources through changes in their terms of trade has grown since 1958 until it is now running at $2½ billion, or nearly half the flow of official aid. These price changes have frustrated the intention of the developed countries to transfer resources to the developing countries, and there are many reasons to suppose that such price changes will continue, unless intervening action is taken.

Intervention in the process of resource transfer could take the form of compensating flows of aid but political and commercial factors play so large a role in the distribution of aid that the prospects of getting full multilateral compensation are remote. In a situation of partial compensation on a bilateral basis not only do some recipients get left out but unit cost to donors is inflated because other developed countries are not contributing. A fully multilateral system of compensating aid upon an automatic basis is in the end indistinguishable from a thorough going commodity agreement.

Finally it has been argued that, although only a few commodities are susceptible to traditional forms of agreement, there are other methods of proven value which could be used in the case of the remaining commodities. Such methods can also be designed to increase efficiency in the Agreement industries and to encourage the changes in economic structure required.

In brief this is the case for the general introduction of commodity schemes for tropical crops[28] on a wide front. Acceptance of these principles would go far to help growth in the developing countries, by providing a secure base for the main items in their commodity trade. While these would be resource costs to such schemes (in the windfall terms of trade effects foregone on tropical agricultural imports), such items constitute a small fraction of total commodity imports in most consuming countries[29] so that their balance of payments effects would be small, and largely, if not wholly, offset by increased sales of exports.[30]

This is a situation in which the same course of action is dictated both in the interests of the developing world and of our own. With the UK share in world exports falling partly because she sells much in the slower growing primary producer countries of the world, even long-term considerations support such policies as a matter of enlightened self-interest.

Notes and references

1 *Instability in Export Markets of Underdeveloped Countries* (1952).
2 *International Economic Instability* (1963).
3 *Export Instability and Economic Development* (1967).
4 The log variance ratio

$$V_{\log} = \left(\frac{\sum \log \frac{X_{t-1}}{X_t} - m}{N} \right)^2$$

Where X_t = export proceeds at time t
m = arithmetic mean of the difference between the logs of X_t and X_{t-1}, X_{t+1} and X_{t+2}, etc.
N = number of years minus 1.

5 Some confirmation of this criticism can be found in a routine series on manufactures in world trade.

Exports of manufactured goods in world trade (1958=100)

	1957	1958	1959	1960	1961	1962	1963	1964	1965	1966
Value ($ billion)	44·7	43·8	47·0	54·0	56·5	60·3	65·2	74·3	83·3	93·0
Index numbers										
Unit value	101	100	99	101	102	102	103	104	106	108
Quantum	101	100	108	122	126	134	145	163	178	196

Source: UN Monthly Bulletin of Statistics, December 1967.

The stability of this series even in the recession of 1958 offers a marked contrast to experience with primary commodities in the same period. See table 3.

6 Coppock *loc. cit.* p. 33.
7 Coppock *loc. cit.* p. 44.
8 Other than minerals and oil.

9 However, even for this peculiar period, a recent repetition of his work
   suggests that he was wrong. For using MacBean's own published data,
   Maizels has found a high correlation when the sample studied was made
   more homogeneous.
10 But see more detailed criticism in Maizels' review of MacBean's book in
   American Economic Review LVIII, June 1968, 575–80.
11 *Trends in International Trade* (1958).
12 Patterns of Trade and Development (1959).
13 *Industrialization and World Trade.*
14 The rationale of this is that you can deflate a commodity flow not a
   difference of two flows where deflators differ. Geary (16) has tested this
   formula against other methods of deflation, e.g. using the general price
   level and finds that there is no significant difference.
15 UN Monthly Bulletin November Table showing the unit value of exports
   of all kinds from and to different groups of countries.
16 Even in the service sector capital costs are high, e.g. in tourism, where a
   modern tourist industry requires international class hotels and systems of
   transport.
17 e.g. donor countries' calculations of commercial self interest.
18 This is in any case not high, when its normal value is adjusted, for the
   high proportion of loans and the effects of bilateral aid and commodity
   aid. For a recent calculation of the real resource transfer through aid
   see G. Colin *Foreign Aid Policies Reconsidered.* OECD Development Centre
   (Paris 1965).
19 This need not be built into an agreement since the same ends can be
   achieved by taxation or multiple exchange rates.
20 Tea is the only one in this list which is a plantation crop in India and
   Ceylon. In East Africa, where output is rising rapidly, it is a peasant crop
   and is now replacing coffee.
21 At UNCTAD II, proposals for tea and bananas went no further than
   support for FAO study groups.
22 See UNCTAD *Commodity Problems and Policies* (1968) Section 14.
   Subsection II. 1. 'Price stabilisation . . . may be achieved by a now
   well-known range of techniques, which can be used singly or in combination, and which may vary with the product.'
23 Price-support schemes for sugar are operated on the basis of a modified
   bilateralism by the USA, the UK, France, Portugal and the USSR, each
   guaranteeing cane-sugar import prices for a specified list of overseas
   countries supplying a quota of their imports.
24 Through the terms of trade effect.
25 See UNCTAD *Commodity Problems and Policies* (1968). A group of
   developed countries (in fact the EEC) put forward two proposals at
   UNCTAD II, the first, a set of general principles upon pricing policy, was
   openly opposed only by the USA and Canada. The second, a proposal for
   the elements of a commodity policy, never reached the table owing to a
   shortage of time for completion of the Agenda. See UNCTAD *op. cit.*
   Section 9. Operational guidelines esp. (d) Also Section 14.
26 Caisses de Stabilisation des Prix. These agencies now operate like Marketing
   Boards in paying producers a stabilised but low price, keeping any surplus
   earned through sales at world prices for development financing.
27 UNCTAD *Commodity Problems and Policies* (1968) Section 7 sub(d).
   (financing of research).
28 Minerals are already sold in world markets through international schemes,
   even if privately financed.
29 Less than 10 per cent of the UK import bill on commodities, for example.
30 In the UK offsetting increases in exports may be expected to exceed the
   extra cost of such commodity imports because of the structure of our
   import trade.

ROBERT M.STERN

International Financial Issues in Foreign Economic Assistance to the Less Developed Countries

The purpose of this paper is to discuss some of the major international financial issues of current importance in the provision of foreign economic assistance to the less developed countries (LDCs). These issues are to be seen against a background of increasing criticism of foreign aid, especially in the United States where the aid proponents have experienced difficulties in convincing Congress that aid is observedly a catalyst to development and that it is in the interests of the United States to become heavily involved *via* the aid programme in the internal affairs of recipient countries. The questioning of foreign-aid commitments in the United States and elsewhere has been reflected in the fact that there have been only modest increases in official aid disbursements especially since 1961. These developments have occurred despite the widely held belief that many LDCs could effectively use more aid. They have also come at a time when there are signs of mounting debt-service requirements that particular LDCs may find hard to meet in the near future.

In what follows, we shall focus in particular in Section I upon the programmes of Development Assistance Committee (DAC) members, giving special attention to the policy issues arising out of bilateralism in aid giving, the emphasis on project financing, tied aid, surplus commodity aid, and special problems created by the increased use of suppliers' credits. We shall then treat briefly in Sections II–IV some of the important financial characteristics of the assistance programmes of the centrally planned economies, policies of the multilateral institutions, and policies of the recipient countries. Attention is directed in Section V to possible new directions in development assistance policies especially with regard to aid tying, suppliers' credits, and debt rescheduling. Some brief concluding remarks are given in Section VI.

I. DAC MEMBER COUNTRIES

The predominance of bilateral assistance

In recent years the DAC countries have disbursed on a bilateral basis about 80 per cent of the total net official flow of long-term financial resources to the LDCs.[1] This percentage would be even greater if account were taken in addition of total net private long-term flows.

This 80 per cent figure is in a sense an overstatement, however, because it does not reflect adequately the influences which international agencies have had on the flow of resources by their sharing of experiences, the studies they have made of development problems and the need for and the utilization of development finance, and the discussions and recommendations they have sparked. These institutions have also played a more direct rôle in affecting bilateral flows by influencing the sizable commitments which have been made in recent years through the activities of aid consortia and in the debt reschedulings which have been arranged for a number of LDCs.

It remains nevertheless that national interests are still and will continue to be reflected significantly in the assistance efforts of donor countries. This is borne out by the preferences which individual donors show for the financing of projects rather than programmes, the frequency with which they tie their aid through procurement restrictions, and the importance especially for the United States of surplus commodity aid, the substantial variation which exists in the terms on which assistance is extended, and the special incentives which are provided to encourage the expansion of exports.

Project and programme assistance

There has been a longstanding preference in both bilateral and multilateral assistance programmes for the financing of specific projects in developing countries. Thus, the preponderance of multilateral commitments is stipulated for project financing. According to the data in table 1, which cover the distribution by purpose of official bilateral assistance programmes, about 31 per cent of bilateral commitments in 1965 was made for capital-project financing. Although about 42 per cent was apparently allocated for non-project (i.e., programme) assistance, it should be pointed out that only 9 per cent was in the form of freely usable foreign exchange. The other 33 per cent evidently reflected in great part United States surplus agricultural commodity shipments. However, since these shipments are to some extent directed to consumption uses that have been especially created in response to the availability of surplus-commodity aid, the recorded contribution to programme finance would appear to be somewhat overstated.

There is a preference for project financing on the part of donors because projects deal with ostensibly tangible investments which produce recognizable returns. They can be subjected therefore to careful costing in terms especially of the amount of foreign exchange which may be necessary to fulfill specific equipment needs and to

TABLE 1   Distribution by purpose of official bilateral commitments, 1965

| Country | Capital project financing | Non-Project Assistance (%) | | | | Cons. and refinancing loans | Other[4] | Total |
		Current expenditure financing	Cash transfers[2]	Current imports financing[3]	Technical cooperation			
Australia	22·6	10·1	53·8	10·5	3·0	—	—	100·0
Austria	—	—	—	93·3	6·7	—	—	100·0
Belgium[1]	4·9	0·4	—	1·3	31·3	0·8	61·1	100·0
Canada	71·5	—	0·2	22·4	5·9	—	—	100·0
Denmark	33·0	—	—	—	31·8	35·2	—	100·0
France	39·7	2·5	16·0	—	40·2	1·4	0·2	100·0
Germany	34·0	—	8·8	15·8	18·8	8·9	13·7	100·0
Italy[1]	46·0	—	5·4	11·6	3·9	31·9	1·2	100·0
Japan	28·5	—	0·4	10·4	2·8	37·0	21·1	100·0
Netherlands	24·2	—	48·7	—	27·0	0·1	—	100·0
Norway[1]	47·4	—	—	—	36·8	—	15·8	100·0
Portugal	—	—	58·4	—	21·0	21·0	—	100·0
Sweden	48·6	—	—	—	51·3[1]	—	—	100·0
Switzerland	75·5	—	6·5	—	18·0	—	—	100·0
United Kingdom	32·3	0·6	23·9	18·6	19·3	5·2	—	100·0
United States	26·4	—	4·0	54·4	13·2	—	2·0	100·0
Total	31·2	0·6	9·0	33·4	17·5	4·3	4·1	100·0

[1] Gross disbursements.
[2] Non-project assistance not directly linked with imports.
[3] Includes contributions in kind and agricultural surplus commodity shipments.
[4] Comprises mainly payments by Belgium of the interest and amortization of the external Congolese debt and reparations payments of Germany, Italy, and Japan.

Source: OECD The Flow of Financial Resources to Less-Developed Countries, 1961–65 (Paris 1967) p. 228.

E

supply technical personnel and other requisites. They may also permit leverage to be exerted on the recipient through the financial discipline which the external financing will involve and by requiring a certain proportion of the investment to be met from local resources. Projects can furthermore be tailored by the donor countries to coincide with their particular export availabilities and at times to further their national prestige.

Project financing may have definite advantages to developing countries for reasons that are similar to some of those just mentioned. But there are drawbacks as well. This is especially the case if projects are defined too narrowly. Insufficient account may be taken therefore of the need for additional resources to finance expansion in other sectors and to satisfy increases generally in demand as income rises. It is also possible that distortions will be created if projects are financed subject to donor-country procurement specifications or to further donor-country prestige, and inadequate attention is given to development priorities, technical skills, and other resource availabilities in the developing country's economy. The reluctance to finance the local costs of projects may produce still further distortions by increasing the capital intensity of investment, forcing the recipient to turn to more costly external financing alternatives, and creating greater pressure on the recipient to resort to deficit financing.

There is a tendency, moreover, for project finance to be concentrated on relatively large investments. The consequence of this may be to retard the expansion of small-scale investment which does not lend itself readily to project financing but which nevertheless contributes importantly to development. It may be mentioned, finally, that the time consumed in project implementation and negotiation may slow down the utilization in the developing country of aid resources in general and thus have a retarding effect on growth.

Because projects have characteristics which lend themselves to discrete financing decisions, they will continue to be the main objects of external development finance. The prerequisite for programme financing is apparently a carefully drafted and consistent plan for the execution and financing of the recipient's development programme. The advantage of such a plan is the assurance that adequate consideration will be given by the recipient to provisions for overall growth, price stability, and balance-of-payments equilibrium. This is something which a project orientation cannot accomplish. The arguments in favour of additional programme assistance are therefore compelling. It is perhaps also worth stressing in this connection that programme assistance would by no means reduce the need for sound project evaluation. If anything, it would increase this need since it would be necessary to look comprehensively at all of the recipient's projects and to appraise the capacity and abilities of the recipient-country agencies that will handle the implementation and financing of the projects.

There has fortunately been increasing recognition on the part of donors and multilateral agencies of some of the limitations of project financing and the merits of and need for additional programme financing in a number of countries. The various aid consortia and consultative groups convened under the auspices of the World Bank (IBRD) and the Organization for Economic Cooperation and Development (OECD) have been influential in this respect. They have furnished a forum in which the provision and design of the resources of the donor countries and international agencies can be brought more effectively to bear in the fulfillment of the capabilities and needs of the LDCs.

Tied aid[2]

The emphasis on bilateralism and project financing has come increasingly to embrace the tying of aid by country source and end use. Thus, it has been estimated that during 1961–3 about two-thirds of the gross bilateral assistance of DAC member countries was contractually tied or otherwise limited.[3] This proportion may actually be higher now in view especially of the more comprehensive tying measures instituted since that time especially in the United States.

Aid-tying restrictions have political roots in the legislative processes in individual countries. These restrictions have been sought not only for administrative reasons but perhaps also to demonstrate that aid meant increases in the country's exports. The increased use of suppliers' credits and other devices to stimulate exports has furthered tying. But in recent years, especially on the part of the United States, aid tying has been extensively broadened because of balance-of-payments difficulties.

The object of United States tying restrictions is to curtail sharply the expenditure of aid proceeds by recipient countries on the export goods of the other more advanced countries. The reason behind this is that when the exports of these countries increased, they would be likely to accumulate additional foreign exchange reserves at the expense of the United States rather than to increase their imports from this country. It should be clear therefore that aid tying on balance-of-payments grounds is a reflection of the inadequacy of the workings of the international-financial mechanism of adjustment for the restoration of payments equilibrium among the more advanced countries.

Since the United States is the main country which has instituted tying on such a broad scale, it is instructive to consider briefly the effects this has had on its balance-of-payments. Thus, Bhagwati, on the basis of some information supplied by Alan Strout, has estimated that aid tying in 1966 may have 'saved' the United States as much as $1·1 billion, which was equal to 39 per cent of total procurement in that year.[4] Bhagwati further estimated that the elimination of tying by all the DAC member countries simultaneously would have resulted in an estimated loss in export proceeds for the United States of about $800 million in 1963 and $688 million in 1964.[5]

These estimates of the foreign-exchange savings of tied aid must of course be interpreted with caution. This is because they were based upon an assumed proportion of 30 per cent representing the balance-of-payments 'gains' from aid tying, and upon the further assumption that untying aid would redistribute exports according to the market shares of DAC countries actually observed in 1962–4. The fact remains nevertheless that the foreign-exchange savings of tied United States aid are substantial and that the removal of tying would result therefore in a significant increase in the United States balance-of-payments deficit. The untying of aid under present conditions would have to be predicated therefore on multilateral action, with the surplus countries especially untying more than their proportionate share of total aid.

Looked at from the standpoints of the world as a whole and the LDCs in particular, there is a definite presumption that aid tying is an inefficient policy. This inefficiency will not be especially serious when the donor country can supply a broad range of goods at or close to world market prices. But the costs of inefficiency will become more substantial as the donor country narrows its range of available goods, becomes less competitive internationally and tolerates explicit or implicit collusion by domestic producers in setting prices for aid-financed goods. The disadvantages to the recipient will vary also depending on its availability of other external resources besides the tied aid. The more limited these other resources, the greater will be the reliance of the recipient on the tied aid and the greater therefore the possibility that this aid may not accord well with the recipient's needs and development priorities.

The excess costs of aid tying will of course vary from country to country. Unfortunately, there is only scattered information on what these costs may actually be in particular circumstances. It is difficult therefore to reach any general conclusion as to the most likely order of magnitude. Thus, for example, Bhagwati has analysed the spreads of bids on competitive tendering from 20 World Bank loans and 3 IDA credits amounting to a total of $200·9 million in the years 1960–6. He measured the percentage of potential excess cost as the ratio of the difference between 'high bids' and 'successful bids' to 'successful bids'. His results indicated an average potential excess cost of 49·3 per cent, and 'that over 31 per cent of the value of contracts awarded . . . were characterized by potential excess cost of over 50 per cent, and 62·9 per cent of the value of contracts awarded were characterized by potential excess cost of over 30 per cent.'[6]

In his pioneering study of aid tying in Pakistan, Ul Haq arrived at an estimate of 12 per cent of excess cost on the basis of a loss of $60 million out of a total annual aid flow of $500 million in 1961–3. This was a relatively low figure which Ul Haq attributed to Pakistan's flexibility in seeking alternative suppliers and the relatively low proportion of tied aid to total aid.[7] In a study of six projects involving transport and harbour equipment undertaken in Iran in 1966–7, Eshag estimated an average excess cost of about 15 per cent on disbursements of $18·9 million. However, since the excess cost on dams and electric-power projects was estimated to be appreciably smaller, Eshag concluded that the average rate of excess cost on total tied aid received by Iran in 1966–7 may have been 10 per cent or less. He attributed Iran's ability to keep down these costs to its success in diversifying aid sources, the negotiation of untied.global credit agreements, and the financing of parts of projects with its own foreign-exchange recourses.[8]

Many more case studies of recipient countries are needed before we could say whether in general the excess costs of aid tying are greater or less than, for example, 10–15 per cent. But whatever the correct percentage, it is clear that the nominal aid figures may substantially overstate the real value of the aid being transferred to the recipient countries.[9] Thus, projects undertaken with tied aid in recipient countries may turn out to be inefficient unless their costs can be written down or some other adjustments made. Moreover, to the extent that the tied aid is furnished in loan rather than grant form, repayment may possibly result in returning to the lender more in real value than was actually received. This may be the case even if the loan is provided on soft terms.[10] Finally, it does not seem completely equitable when loans are tied to ask the recipient to make repayments in freely convertible foreign exchange.

It is clear from the foregoing discussion that really fundamental progress in removing aid-tying restrictions depends upon needed reforms in the international monetary system. Making the system more stable by reducing or eliminating the rôle of the dollar as a reserve currency and establishing a more effective balance-of-payments mechanism of adjustment would obviate the necessity of deficit countries, the United States especially, to resort to such defensive policies as aid tying. There may also be a need in this connection, as will be noted below, for the more advanced countries to reconsider some of their policies of export promotion.

According to the Chairman of the DAC: 'There cannot be said to have been any appreciable progress towards more liberality in aid tying during recent years.[11] Given the pressing needs of the LDCs and the present uncertainties concerning international monetary reform, it may consequently be more fruitful at this stage to deal with the problem piecemeal by seeking to develop a series of individual measures, all with the same purpose of adding flexibility to and reducing the costs of aid procurement to the LDCs.

Surplus commodity aid

Mention has been made in our earlier discussion of the substantial aid transfers of surplus agricultural commodities by the United States especially in connection with its Public Law 480 programmes. The humanitarian aspects of these programmes are certainly laudable in their goals to ameliorate famine and other emergency conditions and in helping to raise consumption standards in many developing countries. The sales of surplus commodities for local currencies under Title I of Public Law 480 have also provided substantial programme-finance benefits to the recipient countries by enabling them to divert scarce foreign exchange to capital-goods imports, to help control inflation, and in some cases to utilize the surplus commodities in conjunction with the expansion of domestic investment.

There have, however, been certain negative influences arising from these programmes in particular instances. Thus, sales for local currency of wheat especially may have caused some trade diversion to the disadvantage of competing exporters, among which were such developing countries as Argentina and the rice exporters of southeast Asia. Also, local currency sales may have depressed the domestic price structure of competing crops, thereby creating disincentives to increases in production and productivity in the recipient country. These disincentives may have been exacerbated, finally, if continued reliance on surplus-commodity imports resulted in the diversion of government policies in the recipient countries away from needed improvements in their agricultural sector.

It is especially noteworthy that in recent years there have been substantial increases in the world demand for grains and a definite trend in United States domestic agricultural policy towards lower price supports which has resulted in significant reductions in surplus stocks. The demand for imported foodstuffs will no doubt continue to increase in the future in LDCs which are experiencing difficulties in expanding domestic agricultural output. There may also be a large potential demand intermittently particularly in the centrally planned economies as a result of vagaries in production due to unfavourable weather conditions. If such increases in demand come at a time when there are relatively poor crops in some of the important LDC producing countries, the resulting squeeze might threaten the continuity of this type of aid. It deserves mention, furthermore, that the United States has amended its Public Law 480 programme to reduce Title I sales for local currencies in favour of new Title IV arrangements which provide for dollar sales. Finally, we can take note of the World Grains Agreement negotiated in mid-1967, during the Kennedy Round, which will involve an annual contribution by the industrialized countries in kind or currency equivalent of 4·5 million tons of wheat to a multilateral food-aid programme.

When we consider the implications of all the foregoing considerations, there are two that stand out especially. The first involves the increasing reliance of many LDCs on imported foodstuffs. This is an issue which must on the whole be dealt with in these countries through programmes aimed at stimulating domestic agricultural output and restraining the rate of population growth. Such programmes take of course a long time to implement, which means that the dependency of many countries on food imports is likely to continue.

The second implication is whether the LDCs will be able to satisfy their food import needs without a substantial drain on their foreign-exchange resources in view of the changes noted in the potential availability of surplus foodstuffs and in the switch from local currency to dollar sales on the part of the United States. The switch to dollar sales means that the grant equivalent of the United States food-aid programme will be reduced and the potential debt-servicing needs of the LDCs increased. It may be, however, that the new multilateral food-aid arrangements will compensate for this change. The possibility of relatively large transitory increases in commercial demands for imports due to crop fluctuations must still be reckoned with by the LDCs, however. Such occurrences might be alleviated by stockpiling in the LDCs themselves or by means of special financial arrangements extended by the donor countries for LDC imports.

Loan terms, suppliers' credits, and problems of debt servicing

The adoption by the DAC in July 1965 of the Recommendation on Financial Terms and Conditions marked an important departure in the aid field by establishing numerical targets for aid terms against which the performances of DAC members could be compared.[12] According to the *1967 Review* (p. 81), in 1966 seven of the fifteen DAC members met the grant test (Australia, Norway, Belgium, France, Canada, Netherlands, and Sweden); the United States and

United Kingdom complied with two of the alternative provisions; Denmark and Germany complied with one of the alternative provisions; and Japan, Portugal, Austria, and Italy did not comply with any of the provisions.

An issue connected closely with that of the average loan terms is the substantial variation which exists in these terms among the various DAC members. This applies not only to official aid commitments but to an even greater extent to both government guaranteed and private non-guaranteed export-credit financing (i.e., suppliers' credits). Thus, it was bearing in mind the significant disparities that exist both in general and with respect to particular recipient countries that the aforementioned recommendation called upon DAC members to harmonize and to soften their terms of assistance where appropriate. The importance of this recommendation lies in the possibility that, if significant disparities are permitted to exist, the spectacle of the harder terms elsewhere may make it difficult for some countries to soften further or perhaps even to maintain existing terms. Moreover, inequities may be created if the hard terms of some donors pre-empt the debt servicing capacity of recipients at the expense of other donors that have provided assistance on soft terms.

This last point may indeed be the crux of the matter of the debt-servicing problems of many LDCs, especially as far as terms of suppliers' credits are concerned. Thus, it is apparent that the debt-service liabilities on guaranteed private export credits are quite substantial for a number of LDCs. This has been due mainly to the rapid growth in credits of more than five years' duration as the industrialized countries have tried to outdo one another in liberalizing credit terms in order to expand their exports and obtain footholds in the markets of many LDCs.[13] It may not be an exaggeration therefore to state that the need in many cases for softer terms on public assistance is to help offset the hard terms that many developing countries must pay on their suppliers' credits.

The statement just made should by no means be construed to denigrate the important role of suppliers' credits in the financing of trade. Nor should this statement be taken as a rationalization which is intended to overlook the mistakes in economic policy in some LDCs that may result in financial crises. The situation is one nevertheless that the LDCs cannot cope adequately with themselves given their pressing needs for capital and their inability to foresee clearly future debt problems or to exercise effective restraint over vested interests, both domestic and foreign.

As far as the donors are concerned, they should consider that they may all be engaged in a game that nobody wins on balance, although private interests may gain when suppliers' credits are converted into public assistance as part of a debt re-scheduling exercise. The time may be at hand therefore to call for restraint among donor countries in extending suppliers' credits to countries that are already over-burdened with debt.[14] Serious attention should also be directed within the donor countries themselves to obtaining more effective co-ordination of the activities of their development-lending and export-credit institutions and thus to reduce the inconsistencies in policies and practices which presently exist.

All debt-servicing problems are by no means associated with sub-stantial accumulation of suppliers' credits, however, for there are some LDCs (e.g., India and Turkey) in which debt-servicing prob-lems stem in large measure from their accumulated official develop-ment-assistance liabilities. In these cases the problems are due more generally to the structural inadequacies of long-run savings and foreign-exchange earnings.[15] The consideration of debt rescheduling should be made to accord therefore with the long-run development criteria that may be most appropriate in these cases for the fulfil-ment of their assistance needs.

II. THE CENTRALLY PLANNED ECONOMIES

Aid provided by the centrally planned economies is characteristically bilateral. It is designed to finance projects and is tied to procurement in the source country. It is common for repayments to be made in kind in the form of the recipient's traditional export goods or occasionally through the export of goods produced from the aid-financed project itself. The foreign-exchange problems of debt servicing familiar in relationships with the developed market econo-mies thus do not arise directly. A further noteworthy feature of the aid activities of the centrally planned economies is the extent to which their assistance embraces all phases of the development of projects through to their final completion. This includes the pro-vision of technical services and the training of local personnel to work on and subsequently to take over the operation of the com-pleted projects. Such practices, if successful, may avoid some of the undesirable effects that utilization of suppliers' credits has provided on occasion in individual recipient countries.

Reliance on the reciprocal tying of aid stems from the concept of 'mutual benefits' which is a principle associated with the aid pro-grammes of the centrally planned economies.[16] This principle has worked out in actuality to encompass both the economic and politi-cal benefits that may accrue to the donor and recipient, although the sharing of the benefits may not be symmetrical. The tying of aid to procurement in the source country has been necessitated by the need to marshal limited supplies of foreign exchange to obtain essential imports. Thus, in this light there would be no aid at all unless it were tied. Aside from foreign-exchange problems, the reason for tying aid on a bilateral basis has been the lack until recently of the convertibility of the currencies of the individual Bloc economies *vis-à-vis* one another. It may be mentioned finally that the practices of tying have been consonant with the physical planning orientation of the donor countries.

The emphasis on bilateralism, project assistance, and the tying of aid would seem to have the same drawbacks mentioned in our earlier discussion, except perhaps for the debt-servicing characteristics which have been noted. There is nevertheless an important degree of uncertainty present in the real loan terms. This arises from the fact that the prices of the aid goods and services and of the goods designated for repayment are based on current world-market prices at the time the aid agreement is negotiated. While these agreements contain safeguards against general inflation and devaluation, they do not offer any guarantee against changes in world prices. The consequence is that if substantial price fluctuations occur, the effect could be to alter significantly the real cost of the loan to both parties. Once this is recognized, the advantage of reciprocal tying becomes somewhat less certain unless there are other compensating factors involved such as those discussed above. This would suggest that it might be fruitful to explore other financing arrangements for repayment that could be operated more flexibly. Such arrangements might now be more feasible than formerly in view of the multilateral-payments balancing that may become more widely used among the centrally planned economies.

The question of the terms of aid of the centrally planned economies also deserves brief comment in connection with the previously discussed debt-servicing problems of some developing countries on account of their outstanding official loan liabilities. The point at issue here is that it is immaterial whether debts are serviced in kind or in foreign exchange. For in both cases, it is clear that the real budgetary cost of debt servicing may be equally burdensome. The centrally planned and the developed market economies thus have a joint interest in debt rescheduling in instances where debt servicing has risen to the point where the development effort is threatened with interruption and retardation.

III. MULTILATERAL INSTITUTIONS

As mentioned earlier, the influences of the multilateral institutions go far beyond merely the recorded magnitudes of their lending and related activities. What is noteworthy in recent years is that their policies and practices have continued to evolve in the light of changing conditions in both donor and recipient countries, and that they have been in the forefront of new departures in the field of assistance.

The world bank

Project financing has long been and will continue to be the main business of the World Bank. However, as the need for additional programme assistance has become increasingly clear, the Bank has allocated a larger amount of its resources for this purpose in particular recipient countries. There are also indications of a greater willingness to finance some proportion of the local costs of projects when the recipient evidently cannot shoulder the entire task. With the coming into existence of the International Development Association (IDA), the Bank has acquired much greater flexibility in establishing the terms of lending by being able to provide funds on blended Bank and IDA terms. Bank influence on the terms of lending has been evidenced further in the joint-financing ventures which it has undertaken in co-operation with donor countries. Finally, the Bank's activities in promoting aid consortia and consultative groups have already borne important results both in increasing the flow of assistance and seeking its more effective utilization.

One of the long established policies of Bank lending has been to direct its financing by means of international competitive bidding to the cheapest sources of supply. Bank financing tied to particular source countries has therefore been ruled out of consideration. While this is a policy with which there can hardly be any quarrel, it has become increasingly clear that the Bank may have to adapt its policy in the light of the conditions which donor countries, the United States in particular, may attach on balance-of-payments grounds to a replenishment and expansion of IDA resources. If it turns out in fact that future pledges to multilateral agencies will contain tying conditions, it will then be imperative for the Bank to develop machinery to administer these pledges so that the excess costs of tying to the recipient countries will be kept at a minimum.[17] By the same token, the Bank might possibly devise ways to exert its influence on aid tying generally to achieve the end just mentioned.

Regional development banks

Another recent innovation which promises to become increasingly important is the organization of regional development banks. The Inter-American Development Bank, which has been in operation since 1960, has already had a significant impact on most aspects of development assistance in Latin America. While the difficulties faced by the Asian and African Development Banks will perhaps yield less readily to solution since the member countries are not as highly developed as those in Latin America, the influence of these banks will nevertheless be important.

The operating characteristics and problems of the regional development banks will in many, but not all, ways parallel those of the World Bank. These banks can therefore profit greatly from World Bank experience and advice. But in catering to the special needs and problems of their regions, they may be able to fulfill a role which otherwise would have gone unplayed. This may involve not only lending activities which cut across national lines, but also activities which will foster the closer integration of these economies. The regional development banks may thus raise problems of aid terms and debt servicing which have a different order of dimension than the more familiar ones which have been considered to date.

Debt servicing and rescheduling

Brief mention may be made finally of the activities of the inter-national Monetary Fund (IMF) and such *ad hoc* entities as the 'Hague', 'Paris' and other creditors' 'clubs' in their concern with debt servicing and debt renegotiation. The majority of these activities has thus been in connection with LDCs that have run into serious balance-of-payments difficulties as a consequence often of lax and improper domestic-economic policies and an associated accumulation of short and medium-term commercial credits which have come due all at once. It has been common practice to approach each case of debt rescheduling on an *ad hoc* basis with fairly short terms and to place great emphasis on the need for domestic reforms to prevent another crisis from occurring. This approach can be defended on the grounds that it is important to avoid creating any presumption that debt rescheduling is something that a recipient country can take for granted.

There is of course much to be said for the view just stated. What may be overlooked, however, is the point mentioned earlier concerning the contribution to the crisis which the more advanced countries may have furnished, especially by their competition in export credits. Some more systematic checks upon the export-credit activities of the more advanced countries may thus help to nip future crises in the bud. The IMF can certainly perform a useful service in this respect through their annual reviews. It may also be fitting in addition to reiterate in the present context the need for more systematic review of cases of impending debt-service problems arising from long-term public assistance loans.

IV. RECIPIENT COUNTRIES

The discussion would not be complete without a few words concerning the effective utilization of development assistance by the recipient countries. Many recipient countries have unfortunately not yet reached the point of being able to cope adequately with the somewhat bewildering array of national, international, and private institutions and mechanisms through which development assistance flows. The problems of recipients are often exacerbated furthermore by the lack of co-ordination among the individual sectors which carry on more or less independent activities involving development finance.

As a consequence of these deficiencies in administration, it is possible that in many countries the costs of assistance may be higher than they would otherwise be. This may be true particularly where tied aid and suppliers' credits are involved and the recipient has not had or taken the opportunity to shop around. Also, the allocation of assistance within the economy may be less efficient as new investment is expanded more in some sectors than in others without adequate consideration of alternative rates of return.

What is required in recipient countries under the circumstances described may be the centralization of responsibility for handling all of the aspects of development finance. It would be possible in this way to build up a staff of trained personnel in each country that would acquire the expertise which is necessary to analyse the various aid offers, negotiate financial terms, provide the link between foreign and domestic-credit institutions, and so on. Some recipient countries have already achieved considerable sophistication in these matters and their experiences and organizations might be studied fruitfully by others. This is also an area of activity in which technical assistance provided particularly through the World Bank and regional development banks could be of great value.

V. NEW DIRECTIONS IN DEVELOPMENT ASSISTANCE POLICIES

It is clear from the survey just completed that there are many difficult problems arising out of existing development assistance policies and practices. Perhaps the most pressing are the problems associated with aid tying, competition among the more advanced countries in the extension of suppliers' credits, and debt rescheduling. Some possibilities for alleviation of these problems have already been suggested or implied in the preceding discussion. It may be useful, however, to spell out these possibilities in somewhat greater detail.

Tied aid

The unilateral reduction of aid tying is a step which donor countries are reluctant to take under present international financial conditions.

This is understandable for countries with balance-of-payments deficits like the United States since unilateral untying might make the deficit larger. But there is no reason why unilateral untying could not be carried out by surplus countries. Of course, such a policy would probably not have immediate effects because of lags in the commitment and disbursement of aid. It is likely, moreover, that since the international competitive position of the deficit country may have deteriorated through time, that country would be forced as part of its balance of payments adjustment to institute measures to improve its position. The point of the unilateral action by the surplus country is therefore to build the effects of untying into the balance of payments adjustment process. Once the country with the initial deficit has moved into equilibrium or into a surplus position, it could then reciprocate the untying action. Aid tying would thus be eliminated gradually provided that the more advanced countries agreed that they would not reinstitute it in the event of future deficits.

Multilateral untying might be considered as an alternative to unilateral untying. But to make it acceptable to deficit countries, it would be necessary to ask the surplus countries to assume a greater share of the commitments. Following the precedent set in the DAC Recommendation on Financial Terms and Conditions, consideration might be given to establishing numerical targets for untying which took into account the balance-of-payments positions of the member countries. This would have the advantages noted above plus providing a standard against which member country performance could be compared.

If it turns out that movement along the foregoing lines is either not feasible or that it would work too slowly, the next best approach would be to seek a series of partial measures, all of which would be designed to operate in the direction of minimizing the excess costs of tying. Such measures might include: (1) subjecting bilateral flows to multilateral review through the activities and organs of the World Bank and the regional development banks; (2) improvements in donor-country aid practices; (3) multilateral purchasing arrangements; and (4) more effective utilization of aid resources in recipient countries.

1. *Multilateralizing influences*
There are already ways in existence by which the World Bank and the regional development banks could further promote a multilateralizing influence on bilateral flows. One of these is through the review process of aid consortia and consultative groups in which the immediate and planned future assistance needs of the recipient

countries are topics for discussion among all the interested parties. Another possibility is through a more widespread use of joint-financing ventures which align the skill and reputation in project analysis and the financial resources of the multilateral institutions with those of individual donor countries. A third way would be to provide some type of international project-costing service that could assist developing countries even when a project was to be financed bilaterally.

It was mentioned above that it is likely that increasing pressure may be brought to bear upon the World Bank especially to alter its longstanding policy against restricted aid commitments. This will be the case if balance-of-payments considerations continue to have a direct bearing upon the foreign-aid programme of the United States, the single largest donor. As noted, the question of aid tying has come up already in connection with the proposed replenishment of IDA resources. Since it would be undesirable and even inequitable to excuse a donor country from its aid commitments on balance-of-payments grounds, aid tying might therefore have to be condoned.

The problem then would be to utilize this tied procurement in order to minimize its inconvenience and the impact of its higher costs on recipient countries. This will be more easily accomplished the more co-operative the donor is in providing a broad list of commodities and services for aid purposes. Since the World Bank would still presumably subject all of its projects to international competitive bidding, it would be in a good position to adjust the volume and terms of its overall resources, including those that were tied, to approximate as closely as possible the cheapest available supply prices for the given investment. This would admittedly be more cumbersome than its regular practices, but there may be no way to avoid it under present balance-of-payments circumstances.

2. *Improvements in donor-country aid practices*

From the standpoint of the donor countries themselves, there are a number of possible measures that they could undertake individually. In cases where it is not already done, administrative procedures could be instituted to oversee the placement of bids domestically and to take steps to assure competitive prices of aid-financed goods. As was mentioned earlier, the question here is not only one of the donor's price quotations being relatively high because of the loss of international competitiveness. Such quotations may be high also because there is a lack of competitiveness in the domestic economy as well and the suppliers in question are able to increase their prices without fear of losing the sale which is to be tied in any case. Assuming that the recipient has no other alternatives, this double tying might therefore impose on it a substantial burden unless the donor country were to take corrective action.

The corrective action of the donor in this case might involve requesting its suppliers to lower their bids to internationally competitive levels, or the donor could adjust the composition of its aid in order to permit a wider choice of goods at competitive prices. If neither of these alternatives was feasible, the donor might be requested to consider releasing the aid funds in question to less costly supply sources in other more advanced countries. However, this might create the problem mentioned earlier concerning the extent to which these other countries would use the increase in foreign exchange to expand imports or to augment their international reserves. The more that particular countries trade normally with one another, the less net drain there might be on the donor's balance of payments. It is possible under these circumstances therefore that the donor might specify certain other supplying countries in which procurement would be permitted when warranted by cost considerations. If these other countries also happened to be in balance-of-payments deficit, an action of this kind could be equilibrating, although it might possibly be objected to on the grounds that it was discriminatory in nature.

Corrective action by the donor could also be taken by making a special grant to the recipient in order to absorb the excess costs due to tying. Or consideration could be given, following the practice of the centrally planned economies and the associated UNCTAD Recommendation A. IV. 4, to tie loan repayments to goods produced in the recipient country. The advantage of a special grant would be to insure that the nominal and real value of the resources made available to the recipient were equivalent. Reverse tying would help to ease the transfer problem of loan repayments. But it is not clear whether the recipient would be relieved of the extra costs of tied aid unless the goods specified for repayment in kind were valued at higher than commercial levels. This might have an important drawback from the donor's standpoint, however, if import of the goods in question displaced domestic production, as could be the case with simple manufactures.

There is also the problem noted earlier that projects financed with tied aid may turn out to be relatively inefficient. Thus, even though a part of the recipient's production was earmarked for repayment purposes, possibly at more favourable than existing market terms, this would only be a partial offset to the inefficiency involved in the project as a whole. It would thus be most desirable if the recipient were able to utilize aid to finance its projects at minimum costs and to realize income both at home and abroad through the sale of efficiently produced goods and services. A special grant to compensate for the excess costs of tying would thus be preferable to reverse tying if it permitted the excess costs in question to be written off.

3. Multilateral purchasing arrangements

A logical extension of the release procedure mentioned in the preceding section might be to develop triangular arrangements in which the donor would specify that its aid be used for procurement in another presumably low-cost country against an equivalent amount of purchases by this other country in the donor's market. The main difficulty with this idea is that it would present the same kind of problem as in direct tying. That is, if the triangular arrangement resulted in the other country switching some of its regular imports from the donor to a different supply source, the donor's balance of payments would be affected adversely to some extent.

An alternative which is similar in principle to the triangular arrangement would be for a donor that was a member of a regional economic grouping to permit the recipient to use the donor's assistance in whatever one or more of the other member countries that happened to be the cheapest source of supply.[18] Such a proposal would work best if the comparative cost structures differed significantly among the member countries themselves, and especially if they carried on a major part of their trade with one another and followed common policies, including multilateral payments balancing at least within the regional grouping.

Of the two major groupings comprising donor countries, the conditions favourable to multilateral purchasing arrangements would appear to be approximated more closely by the Council of Mutual Economic Assistance (COMECON) rather than by the European Economic Community (EEC). This is because the EEC members carry on a substantial part of their trade with outside countries. The EEC members also do not follow as yet completely uniform domestic and international economic policies. In view of these considerations and the fact that they require payments imbalances to be settled mainly in dollars and gold, multilateral purchasing arrangements could result in undesired balance-of-payments effects both within the EEC itself and with respect to outside countries.

In exploring the feasibility of multilateral purchasing arrangements within COMECON, consideration might also be given more generally to multilateral balancing vis-à-vis individual LDCs. These arrangements could conceivably be broadened to permit greater flexibility in the spending by LDCs of bilateral balances within COMECON and by COMECON members within particular LDCs.

F

4. *More effective utilization of aid by recipients*

It is obviously in their own interest for the recipient countries to allocate their foreign-exchange and foreign-assistance resources as efficiently as possible. This is not only a question of the careful preparation and implementation of projects, but also one of co-ordination among the various sectors and institutions concerned with development and its financing in each country. The more successful the recipients are in locating the cheapest sources of supply for the financing of their development needs, the better off they will be. Such success may admittedly make the aid-tying arrangements of the donor countries more difficult to administer on account of the substitutions which the recipients may arrange in their imports both as to composition and source. This process should be looked upon, however, as a balancing rather than a conflict of interests between recipient and donor. It will therefore require both co-operation and understanding.

Suppliers' credits

The problems created by the increased reliance on suppliers' credits by many LDCs must be recognized to be the joint responsibility of these countries themselves, the more advanced countries, and the appropriate multilateral institutions. It is difficult to formulate general principles to deal with these problems because of the wide variations in individual circumstances which exist in both lending and borrowing countries. There is agreement nevertheless on the desirability in general for LDCs to set realistic limits on the amount of credit which they can hope to service when the time comes, for the more advanced countries to co-operate in the exchange of information and jointly to establish norms for credit terms and amounts to suit the debt position and needs of individual borrowing countries, and for the multilateral institutions, the World Bank and IMF in particular, to keep continually in touch with all parties concerned and to use their influence in dealing with problems as they may arise.

The annual IMF consultations and the periodic meetings of the various aid consortia and consultative groups should serve to keep these matters under continual review. More concretely, the possibilities should be explored of a more systematic linking of World Bank financing with that of equipment credits which are largely a national affair at present. The Bank's expertise in project evaluation and knowledge of individual country needs would be brought to bear upon the technical suitability and credit terms on which the equipment was to be financed. This combination of Bank finance and equipment credits, which normally are government guaranteed, would be advantageous moreover to the extent that it enhanced the marketability of the securities underwritten for the given financing.

Debt rescheduling

The question of debt rescheduling is also one that is best dealt with in the context of the situation facing individual countries. As was mentioned earlier, most of the cases of debt rescheduling have been handled thus far on an *ad hoc* basis. However, since the debt-servicing problems of a number of borrowing countries are becoming increasingly apparent,[19] it might be worthwhile to determine if any criteria can be formulated by the lending countries which will be helpful in coping with these problems. Consideration of criteria might include a review of the reschedulings that have taken place in recent years, both as to overall terms and the distribution of the sharing of burdens by individual lending countries. It might also be fruitful to carry out some theoretical exercises under assumed conditions in order to examine the impact of various kinds of rescheduling, especially when the problem is one of servicing long-run liabilities rather than one of dealing with the excessive accumulation of short and medium-term obligations.

There is in addition apparently a need for earlier identification of impending problems and communication among the interested parties. This is an area again in which the aforementioned groups and periodic consultations can be helpful. The IMF in particular could play an important role in furthering the development of an advance warning system that would bring problems to the attention of the lending countries before a crisis stage is reached.

VI. CONCLUSION

The suggestions just made may no doubt appear to be anticlimatic and possibly open to the criticisms that they are unrealistic and in any case will not accomplish very much. It can be argued therefore that what is of the utmost importance is to keep attention focused on the most pressing issue of all, which is to increase the volume of assistance to the LDCs. Thus, the advanced countries should be badgered about their having continually fallen short of the one per cent aid target (based on GNP) and that they should take measures to soften their terms of aid. These countries can be urged, moreover, to channel more of their assistance through multilateral institutions and to give serious consideration to new financing arrangements such as the Horowitz proposal for interest-rate subsidies and the World Bank scheme for supplementary financing.[20] These are laudable objectives, of course, given the pressing needs of the LDCs for capital assistance and import financing and the impending seriousness of debt-servicing problems in many countries.

The fact remains nevertheless that the donor countries have shown little or no inclination in recent years towards increasing substantially the volume of aid flows to the LDCs. This head-in-the-sand attitude on the part of the donor countries is to be deplored. Hopefully, with the settlement of the Vietnam conflict and the calming down and eventual reform of the international monetary system,[21] the attitude towards increased aid flows may become more favourable. There is no guarantee that this will happen, however, particularly if countries like the United States become preoccupied in trying to resolve their own domestic problems. In such an event, it will become imperative to seek greater efficiency in both donor and recipient countries as far as aid giving and utilization are concerned. This is admittedly not a very dramatic prospect, but it may represent the only real choice open in the immediate future.

Acknowledgments

This paper is in part an outgrowth of work on the terms of aid completed in the summer of 1966 while serving as a consultant to the United Nations Conference on Trade and Development (UNCTAD). The latter phases of research were carried on with financial assistance from the University of Michigan's Ford Programme in International Organization. I would like especially to thank Sidney Dell, Director of the New York Office of the UNCTAD, for his encouragement of my efforts and his staff for their kind co-operation in providing working facilities and obtaining documents. I also wish to acknowledge helpful comments on an earlier version of this paper received from members of the Research Seminar in International Economics at The University of Michigan. The views expressed in this paper are my own and not those of any organization with which I have been and presently am affiliated.

Notes and references

1 For further details, see Organization for Economic Cooperation and Development (OECD) *Development Assistance Efforts and Policies of the Members of the Development Assistance Committee, 1967 Review* (September 1967) p. 13.
2 For a comprehensive review of the main issues involved here, see Jagdish N. Bhagwati *The Tying of Aid* UNCTAD, TD/7/Supp. 4 (1 November 1967).
3 OECD *Development Assistance Efforts and Policies, 1965 Review* p. 90. It is noteworthy that this estimate is substantially greater than is implied by the estimates for individual DAC members given in OECD, *The Flow of Financial Resources to Less-Developed Countries, 1961–1965* (Paris 1967) p. 113.
4 Bhagwati *op. cit.* p. 45.
5 Bhagwati *op cit.* p. 48.
6 Bhagwati *op. cit.* p. 33.
7 Mahbub Ul Haq, 'Tied Credits – A Quantitative Analysis', in John H. Adler (ed.), *Capital Movements and Economic Development* (New York 1967) pp. 331–2. Bhagwati *op. cit.* p. 35 has argued that Ul Haq's estimate may be too low because insufficient account has been taken of the possibility of monopolistic pricing of aid-financed goods by donor countries and limited substitution possibilities among supplying countries.

8 Eprime Eshag *Study of the Excess Cost of Tied Economic Aid Given to Iran in 1966/67* UNCTAD, TD/7/Supp. 8/Add. 2 (13 December 1967).
9 See John Pincus *Costs and Benefits of Aid: An Empirical Analysis* UNCTAD, TD/7/Supp. 10 (26 October 1967), for some calculations of the reductions in the real amounts of aid transfers to the LDCs on account of tying. For example, assuming a 12 per cent discount rate, taken to represent the marginal rate of return to domestic investment in the LDCs as a group, and a rate of excess cost on aid tying equal to 15 per cent, Pincus estimated (p. 35) that the 'grant equivalent' of the official borrowing commitments of 39 LDCs (for which World Bank data exist) was only 31·6 per cent of the nominal value in 1964 and 32·3 per cent in 1965.
10 For example, if the tying of aid were to involve an excess cost of the project equal to 50 per cent over world market prices, this would more than offset the transfer contained in a ten-year, interest-free loan repayable in full at maturity and discounted at a 4 per cent alternative cost of capital, or a fifteen-year, interest-free installment loan discounted at 5 per cent. See Harry G. Johnson *Economic Policies Toward Less-Developed Countries* (Washington 1967) p. 81.
11 OECD *Development Assistance Efforts and Policies, 1967 Review* p. 87.
12 According to OECD *op. cit.* p. 80, the targets were 'that DAC Members should either:
   (*a*) provide 70 per cent or more of their commitments in the form of grants; *or*
   (*b*) (i) provide 81 per cent of total commitments as grants or loans at 3 per cent interest charges or less;
      (ii) provide 82 per cent of total commitments as grants or loans with repayment periods of 25 years or more;
      (iii) attain a weighted average grace period of 7 years.'
13 Discussion of the policies and problems arising with suppliers' credits can be found in World Bank *Suppliers' Credits from Industrialized to Developing Countries* (Washington 1967), and United Nations *Export Credits and Development Financing* 67.II.D.1 (New York 1967).
14 The situation with respect to suppliers' credits has been described in The World Bank and IDA *Annual Report, 1966/67* p. 32, as follows: '. . . on the whole, suppliers' credits have played a useful role in development finance, enabling creditors to increase exports of equipment and providing debtors an additional source of finance for investments. In some countries, however, their excessive use has led to unduly high debt-service payments because of maturities considerably shorter than warranted by the country's position. The ready availability of such credits has sometimes encouraged the diversion of scarce resources into low priority projects. In a few extreme cases, the burden of servicing such debt has contributed to financial crises which have required rescheduling operations (e.g., Ghana and Indonesia in 1966; Argentina, Brazil, Chile and Turkey in previous years). Some debt crises have had adverse effects on the credit-worthiness of the countries concerned and thus on their access to foreign finance. The assumption of excessive credits has not been the sole responsibility of the debtor countries; export promotion among creditor countries has often led to the provision of excessive amounts of such credit on terms inconsistent with the debt-servicing capacity of the debtor countries.'
15 See IDA *op. cit.* p. 31.
16 For a discussion of this principle, see United Nations *World Economic Survey* 1965 (New York 1966) ch. IV.
17 According to a World Bank release dated 18 January 1968, the proposed amount of IDA replenishment has been set at $1,200 million, payable in three annual instalments of $400 million each to begin in the fiscal year ending 30 June 1969. It is envisaged that the IDA policy of obtaining competitive international tenders will be continued. But in view of the United States balance-of-payments difficulties, IDA will call only that

portion of the United States contribution required to finance procurement in the United States. If this proposal is accepted, it will be interesting to see whether the World Bank will in fact call the entire United States contribution, even though it is on a tied basis.

18 A rather different alternative might be for the donor to direct his aid in order to foster the integrated development of a number of recipient countries, all of whom had high feedback ratios in their trade *vis-à-vis* the donor. Such a policy would evidently have a goal other than that of obtaining the cheapest supply prices since some margin of protection might be required to make it effective. It is conceivable nevertheless that this protection might justify itself in the long run.

19 Projections of debt service for 1970 and 1975 are to be found in UNCTAD *The Outlook for Debt Service: Report by the UNCTAD Secretariat* TD/7/Supp. 5 (31 October 1967).

20 The Horowitz proposal envisages an organization like the World Bank floating issues at commercial rates in private capital markets and making these funds available to the LDCs on essentially IDA terms. The interest subsidy involved would then be met through donor-country contributions to the IDA. For additional discussion, see UNCTAD *The Horowitz Proposal: Study by the UNCTAD Secretariat* TD/7/Supp. 11 (6 December 1967).

The World Bank scheme for supplementary financing is designed to deal with problems arising from unforeseen export shortfalls which cannot be adequately dealt with by short-term balance-of-payments measures and which threaten to disrupt development programs. For a balanced evaluation of this scheme, see UNCTAD *Supplementary Financial Measures: Final Report of the Intergovernmental Group on Supplementary Financing as adopted by the Group at its third session held at Geneva from 30 October to 13 November 1967* TD/33 (16 November 1967).

21 The big question at the moment is whether and when the new plan for Special Drawings Rights (SDR) will be implemented. It should be emphasized that creation of SDR is intended primarily to ensure an adequate growth of reserves over time for both the industrial countries and the LDCs. The LDCs will receive the SDR in proportion to their IMF quotas, which should lessen to some extent the seriousness of balance-of-payments constraints upon their development. The assurance of adequate reserves in the industrial countries will also be of benefit to the LDCs insofar as rapid expansion is sustained in the level of world trade and there is no necessity to resort to ad hoc balance-of-payments restrictions which affect development aid. It is conceivable of course that the creation of SDR could be linked organically with the provision of additional development aid. But it is doubtful that this is what the industrial countries have in mind. International monetary reform through the activation of the plan for SDR is not likely therefore to lead to an immediate and large increase in the flow of development aid to the LDCs.

W.T.NEWLYN

Monetary Analysis and Policy in Financially Dependent Economies

I shall start by specifying the characteristics which define a financially dependent economy in the sense in which I am using that term. These are as follows:

(i) a high proportion of income arising from exports;
(ii) a high proportion of investment financed from external sources;
(iii) financial institutions based on an external financial centre;
(iv) the absence of both capital market and money market.

These characteristics are present in most of the small developing countries but they are most acute in the ex-colonial countries. In this paper I propose to consider the implications of these characteristics firstly for the type of analysis to be used in explaining monetary behaviour and secondly for the formulation of monetary policy.

Let us start from the traditional Keynesian income-determination model:

$$\Delta Y = \frac{\Delta I}{s+t+m}$$

where Y=income; I=investment; s, t and m=the propensities to save, to pay tax and to import.

The first general qualification that has to be made is that, whereas in this simple multiplier formula appropriate in a developed economy the base of the multiplier is domestic investment, in economies such as we are now discussing the domestic investment element is much less important as a determinant of income and pride of place is taken by the value of exports. This in itself, is not significant for the manner in which we make our analysis; we can easily substitute exports for investment in our income-determination model. Nor does it affect the type of analysis that investment is largely externally financed, for it does not matter from the point of view of income-determination where the money comes from. On the leakage side it is not savings which we must stress but imports; the divorce between savings and investment which is the basis of the Keynesian investment/savings equilibrium does not exist in this kind of economy. The introduction of an import leak does not radically alter the model itself but it does significantly alter the value of the multiplier when applied to Investment.

This is not simply because the value of the marginal propensity to import is high; this is so in many developed economies. More important is the fact that in an economy in which there is no production of producers' goods, a high proportion of any investment expenditure is *initially* absorbed by expenditure on imports. Thus the domestic base of the multiplier is not equal to the total initial expenditure but is equal to the initial expenditure minus that part which is directly spent on imports:

$$\frac{(1-x)\Delta I}{s+t+m}$$

where x is the direct import-content ratio.

The remaining domestic expenditure which is the base of the multiplier may be less than half the total. Combine this with a high marginal propensity to import and, even with fairly low values of the propensity to pay tax and the propensity to save, the value of the domestic multiplier may well be no more than unity.

This formulation of the multiplier analysis is general for any but a closed economy but is much more important in the special case in which a high proportion of any investment expenditure goes on imported producer goods. This is presumably the reason why introductory text books, in their income-determination analysis, implicitly assume a closed economy. This formulation of the reduced-base multiplier fits into the general multiplier pattern in which changes in exports cause an initial income impact equal to the increment in exports; changes in disposable income cause an initial impact of $(1-s)$ times the increment in disposable income; changes in investment-expenditure cause an impact of $(1-x)$ times the increment in expenditure where x is the direct import content in such expenditure.

This reduced-base multiplier is therefore consistent with the general Keynsian model and there is no significant difference in type of analysis. It does, however, introduce a significant difference between the value of the multiplier associated with investment expenditure as between a highly developed economy with its own capital goods industries and a developing economy which has no capital goods industries.

Turning to a similar modification in the monetary field there is a similar difference to take into account. If we regard the expansion of credit as expenditure-generating this has no effect on the calculation of the bank multiplier in a closed economy because the expenditure of a bank loan does not affect the reserves of the banking system. The general form of the multiplier is therefore the conventional text book one:

$$\Delta D = \frac{1}{a+b}\Delta C$$

where D = total bank deposits, C = the cash base, b, a = the cash/deposit ratio of the banks and public respectively.

For an open economy, however, we should add the *external* drain due to direct and indirect expenditure on imports resulting from the credit expansion. The formula for the bank multiplier taking this external drain into account is:

$$\frac{1}{a+b+\left[X+\dfrac{m(1-x)}{s+t+m}\right]}.$$

As would be expected, it is considerably lower in value than that relating to a closed economy. Indeed, only at levels of the variables which are unlikely to obtain in the kind of economy we are examining is the coefficient greater than one. The range of values of this coefficient for various combinations of the direct import-content ratio, the sum of the domestic leaks, and the marginal propensity to import is shown in table 1, based upon a typical total cash to deposits ratio of 0·4.

TABLE 1   Values of the coefficient of expansion

x	$s+t$	m	c
0·1	0·1	0·1	1·03
0·1	0·1	0·5	0·79
0·1	0·5	0·1	1·45
0·1	0·5	0·5	1·03
0·5	0·1	0·1	0·85
0·5	0·1	0·5	0·75
0·5	0·5	0·1	1·00
0·5	0·5	0·5	0·85

x = direct import-content of expenditure
s, t, m = marginal propensities to save, pay tax and import
c = coefficient of expansion (or bank multiplier)

Does this mean that banks are reduced to intermediaries rather than institutions capable of creating money? I think the answer to this is no. In the first place it is quite clear that no bank manager conducting his ordinary business is going to calculate the complicated repercussions of his decision to lend, so that we must assume he will act exactly as he is assumed to act in the general model. But we have incorporated into the general model the expenditure-generating effects of the credit creation and have restricted the analysis to a comparative static statement of the effect (*ceteris paribus*) on the reserves. We must take care not to double-count the expenditure associated with the expansion of credit. If this expenditure is consistent with a balanced external position, the effect of the isolated increment in bank lending coincides with that in a closed economy. However, the fact that this is a special case rather than the general rule has significant implications for monetary policy and for the assessment of the optimum rate of monetary expansion.

So far we have considered only the 'open economy' characteristic of our economy and we have now to consider the effects of 'financial dependence'. Here we have to keep in mind two questions. The first is 'are the domestic leaks appropriate ?' The second is 'what monetary effects follow from the expenditure decisions of the Keynesian model ?'

First, let us look at the investment-saving relationship. We start by considering the characteristic features of indigenous firms in these economies. The typical situation is that of small-scale operation in which investment is financed from retained profits and in aggregate there is probably little discrepancy between the current rate of money saving, and the current rate of investment expenditure, while close contact within communities generally ensures the absence of idle balances. Such idle balances as do arise tend to be transferred to the external money market.

Turning next to consider foreign firms, the absence of a domestic money market causes their surpluses to be exported and their deficits to be financed by imported funds. From this it follows that changes in the relationship between investment and savings are reflected in a corresponding change in the quantity of money. This contrasts with the normal Keynesian model in which changes in expenditure are reflected in changes in the velocity of circulation of money.

We turn next to a consideration of the relationship between government expenditure and taxation. Most of these governments are very hard pressed and the tendency is for expenditure to press hard on tax-receipts. But, to the extent that there are surpluses, these are reflected in increases in external balances, while deficits are financed by decreases in external balances, foreign borrowing or domestic monetary expansion. In all cases there is a corresponding change in the quantity of money.

Finally, we have the relationship between exports and imports and here, in common with other types of economy, it is clear that any change initiated from either will be reflected in a corresponding change in the money supply.

To summarise we have three autonomous determinants: exports, net capital inflow and domestic credit creation; the sum of which we shall refer to as Q which we define as gross money increment, being the total inflow into the money supply over any particular period. The dependent variable in the system which constitutes the only leakage in the income-generating circuit is expenditure on imports, which also constitutes the only leak from the money supply. The conclusion of this analysis is that the velocity of circulation of money must be constant and that income and imports can be regarded as time lagged functions of Q.

This is, in fact, the basis of the Polak model first set out in *International Monetary Fund Staff Papers*.[1] But, whereas Polak *assumes* constancy of the velocity of circulation of money and applies his model to all kinds of economy, irrespective of their degree of openness or financial dependence, my contention is that this constancy of velocity *results from* the economic and financial structure of many developing countries. Although, therefore, I do not accept the applicability of the Polak model as a general case, it seems to me highly relevant to the economies whose characteristics correspond with those I have described. One of the great advantages of the model is that it makes the amount of monetary credit creation explicit and is couched in terms of monetary flows which are familiar concepts to bankers, both central and commercial.

Lest the orthodox Keynesians should throw up their hands in horror at a return to the quantity theory, let me make quite clear that there is no quantity theory hypothesis in this model. The constant velocity postulate is not a reflection of a propensity to hold money in relation to the level of income like that in 'Cambridge K', it is simply a reflection of structural factors, such as the frequency of and interrelationships between payments, combined with a financial and economic structure which substitutes changes in the quantity of money for changes in velocity.

This proposition, deduced from the characteristics of the economies is well borne out in East African monetary statistics in that the *marginal* velocity of total money (currency held by the public plus total commercial bank deposits) has remained remarkably constant. The regression equation for money on income for the period 1956 to 1965 is:

$$M = 44\cdot32 + 0\cdot25Y \qquad R^2 = 0\cdot89$$

This combines a stable marginal velocity of four with a large constant giving a much lower average velocity of 2·8. This constant represents inert balances (especially currency hoards). The important point is that it *is* inert and expenditure variations are not reflected in transfers between the active and idle components.

It must be stressed that this monetary presentation does not in any way constrain the expenditure decisions which are the basis of the general Keynesian model but that, in the special case of the financially dependent economy, these are reflected in variations in the money supply not in variations in its velocity. Indeed, far from being a version of the quantity theory, the Polak model is essentially Keynesian in its income determination characteristics. Income is determined unambiguously by the marginal propensity to import and the level of Q, thus corresponding with the simple Keynesian model of the determination of income by the marginal propensity to save and the level of investment.

We are now in a position to consider how this model works out in practice. We distinguish first between an increase in exports or in net capital inflow on the one hand and an increase in domestic credit creation on the other. Let us first consider a once-and-for-all monetary injection resulting from exports or capital inflow.

A once-and-for-all increment in exports or capital inflow will cause:
  (i) a temporary increase in money income;
 (ii) a temporary increase in imports equal in size to the increase in exports; and
(iii) a temporary increase in the money supply and the external reserves.

Here we have the simple working out of the Keynesian multiplier in terms of exports and the propensity to import, the system reverting to its original equilibrium having generated additional imports equal to the additional increase in exports and thus extinguishing the temporary gain to foreign exchange reserves.

This is sharply distinguished from the result of a once and for all increment in money created by the banking system. Although the effects on income and the stock of money are identical, there is no gain to the foreign exchange reserves as in the case of exports or capital inflow and hence the induced loss of reserves is a net reduction. This is the equivalent in terms of the Polak model of the limiting case of the earlier formulation of the income and bank multipliers; that is to say it is the limiting case in which the domestic leaks are both zero since the reserve loss tends to equality with the initial injection of money as the domestic leaks tend to zero.

Let us consider the effect of a lasting increase in exports or in net capital inflow (that is to say a change in the rate of export receipts or in the rate of inflow of capital) and compare this with a lasting increase in the rate of credit expansion.

A lasting increase in exports or capital inflow will result in:
  (i) a permanent increase in the level of money income as
      determined by the marginal propensity to import;
 (ii) an increase in the rate of imports equal to the increase in
      the rate of exports;
(iii) an increase in the quantity of money and in the foreign
      exchange reserves of an amount depending on the time-lag
      between imports and gross money increment, Q.
In the case of a lasting increase in the rate of credit expansion the
effects on income, imports and the money supply would be the same
as in the preceding case but *there would be a net decrease in reserves
equal to Q minus the increase in the stock of money*. In our comparative static formulation we should have to insert a domestic leak in
the form of accumulating active balances.

The determinants of the time-lag of imports on Q are the marginal
propensity to import and the marginal ratio of money to income.
Thinking of the adjustment through time as the conventional text-
book step-function multiplier process, the propensity to import is
the height of each step and the ratio of money to income is the
interval between steps, or the horizontal distance of each step.

From this it should follow that calculated values of income and
imports can be obtained for any country by applying to the actual
Qs over any period, coefficients derived from the appropriate values
of the import and money ratios of the particular country. Polak has,
in fact, worked out these coefficients for a wide range of values of
the import and money ratios and a reduced set of those for the
calculation of imports is given in table 2. This shortcut to the full

TABLE 2   Polak coefficients for determination of $M(0)$

Velocity	Import ratio	$Q(0)$	$Q(-1)$	$Q(-2)$	$Q(-3)$	sum
2	0·10	0·13	0·15	0·12	0·10	0·50
	0·50	0·44	0·31	0·14	0·06	0·95
3	0·10	0·17	0·21	0·15	0·12	0·65
	0·50	0·53	0·33	0·10	0·03	0·99
4	0·10	0·21	0·25	0·17	0·12	0·75
	0·50	0·60	0·32	0·06	0·01	0·99
5	0·10	0·24	0·29	0·19	0·11	0·83
	0·50	0·65	0·30	0·04	0·01	1·00
6	0·10	0·27	0·32	0·18	0·10	0·87
	0·50	0·70	0·28	0·02	0·00	1·00

application of the Polak model thus boils down to applying co-efficients representing a distributed time-lag to the actual values of Q for any period.

Apart from the difficulties of identifying the values of Q (which mainly arise in connection with the measurement of net capital inflow) there are ambiguities about the appropriate concepts to be used in connection with the import and money ratios. Taking the latter first we run into the difficulty of defining the money stock. I confess to a vested interest in a definition which, so far as I know, has not been challenged, but which does not conform to the convention of international monetary statistics which is used by Polak.[2] I don't want to argue here which is right – I simply draw attention to the possibility of conflicting interpretation.

The next ambiguity is whether we should take average or marginal velocity. In the first of the articles expounding the model Polak takes average velocity but this seems wrong. Of course if you make your constant velocity assumption relate to average velocity then marginal and average will be equal, but it seems unnecessary to make this more restrictive assumption. In the second article this point is raised but is dismissed on the grounds that no example of a persistent discrepancy between average and marginal velocity has been encountered in the research. East African data *does* show such a discrepancy. If we combine these two factors using East African data and taking the extreme limits of the definition of the money stock and the two alternative versions of marginal and average velocity we get a range of possibilities for the money/income ratio from 2·8 to 6·5.

The same problem of 'marginal versus average' applies to the propensity to import. Again in his first article Polak uses the average relationship, whereas it would seem to me that the marginal propensity is appropriate. In the second article the implications of discrepancy between marginal and average propensities is discussed and it is shown that a straight substitution in the formula of the model is all that is required. Indeed in the country study given for Norway, the marginal propensity is used instead of the average. Which is used can, of course, make a considerable difference. For East Africa the marginal relationship over the period 1956–65 was 0·24 while the average for the same period was 0·42.

A glance at the sensitivity of the coefficients in table 2 to the values of the money and income ratios will reveal the futility of selecting the time-lag on this basis given the large range of interpretation of these ratios. Nevertheless, the Polak coefficients do merge from the model as functions of the basic determinants of the time lag and it is convenient to use them simply as an ordered set of three-year distributed lags with which to determine the 'best fit' time-lag, without regard to the particular values of the import and money relationships to which it corresponds, provided that it falls within the feasible range.

The specific application for which I have used the Polak model was an attempt to estimate the accuracy of the projections of imports in Uganda's *Second Five Year Plan*. The method consisted of applying the model to the actual data of a preceding five-year period (requiring data over an eight-year period because of the three-year time-lag) in order to ascertain the best fit coefficients of Q for the calculation of imports and then applying that optimum coefficient to the values of Q stated or implied in the five-year plan, after incorporating specific amounts of monetary expansion. Unfortunately I was not able to include this version in my published study because of the absence of published balance of payments estimates for Uganda. Two unpublished estimates were available to me on a confidential basis and these I used in the manner I have just outlined. For the published version I had to make do with an unsatisfactory makeshift; I calculated the optimum time-lag from East African data for the period 1956–65 and used that. The justification for so doing, if it can be justified, was that Uganda stands basically mid-way between Kenya and Tanzania in its economic characteristics and that an East African aggregate might not be too misleading as applied to Uganda.

In both cases the predictive value of the model when applied to past data was disappointing. In all cases there were very high correlations between the actual values of imports and the values calculated from any coefficients falling within the range of interpretation of the money and income ratios; but no correlation of first differences was significant. This gave no basis for selection and I adopted a rather crude criterion: namely the sum of the deviations equal to zero for the period under examination. Using this rather crude technique, both the Uganda based versions and the East African based version predicted imports lower than those estimated for the five-year period in the plan, so that I was fairly happy about incorporating that conclusion into the study. It was, I regret to say, the only optimistic conclusion I came to in assessing the financial feasibility of the plan which, in common with many others, contained no *financial* planning whatever.

I use this particular application as an illustration of the simplicity with which the Polak model can be applied given the availability of reasonable balance of payments figures. My interest in it was to demonstrate simple quantitative technique which would make credit creation explicit in a context in which the three newly established banks of East Africa were feeling their way in developing a basis for monetary policy. I think it is probable that the model could be improved so as to overcome the imperfect prediction of imports to which I referred.

I turn now to policy. I have for long been persuaded that the constraints imposed on credit creation by the type of financial and economic structure that I have described are very narrow, but the advantage of the analysis that I have been elaborating seems to me to lie in the fact that both the amount of credit creation and the constraints are made explicit. In my view monetary policy in such economies has little chance of doing much to offset fluctuations due to variations in primary export earnings. I am a strong advocate of marketing boards using stabilisation techniques providing that their operations are integrated into overall economic policy and providing that they are not used as instruments of taxation. I also favour fiscal stabilisation techniques for this purpose. In both cases, however, the constraint on maintaining domestic prices at a higher level than export values comes back to the availability of surplus foreign exchange reserves.

In spite of the exclusion of monetary policy from this very important field I would maintain that monetary management in the less developed economies of the type we are considering is of crucial importance. It is not only in Latin America that monetary expansion in the post-war period has been excessive. I believe it has also been excessive in most of the English speaking African countries (even in East Africa where the Currency Board persisted up to 1966) whereas the French speaking African countries have been excessively restricted by the continued ultimate domination of Paris. Expansion in the English speaking countries has resulted from a combination of central banks lending to their governments (except in Rhodesia) and a massive expansion of commercial bank credit through a rapid spread of bank coverage and the absorption of post-war liquidity. This phase has now come to an end with both central banks and commercial banks fully- or over-extended. A combination of this circumstance with over-optimistic development planning creates intense pressures for solving the government's financial constraint by means of credit creation. When the effect of the resulting excessive demand has its impact upon imports and reserves are not available, the inevitable reaction is rigorous import restriction, as in Ghana, with disastrous results.

One of the difficulties which has always complicated monetary policy (not only in developing countries) has been that of specifying a criterion for the 'right' rate of monetary expansion. This is because the results of monetary expansion form the justification for further monetary expansion. If the government cannot raise tax-revenue fast enough to meet its increasing expenditure it has to create money; ex-post the money supply has simply been adjusted to the increased demand for it. If the IMF forbids (say) Argentina to expand its money supply further, the government has to default on paying its civil servants and contractors. In economies in which the major impact of excess demand falls on imports it seems to me that the difficulty of specifying the necessary criterion for control of monetary expansion is greatly reduced. Moreover it is only in the Polak model that this criterion emerges clearly.

It follows from the characteristic which defines the model, that over a period, gross money increment resulting from exports and capital inflow will be offset by gross money decrement due to imports with about a three-year time-lag. This is simply the self-balancing mechanism of the multiplier working itself out. From this it follows that the effect of exports and capital inflow is zero both for reserves and the money supply. The observed change in reserves must therefore be equal to the gross credit creation during the period minus the increment in the monetary supply. In accounting identities this is simply to say that the assets of the banking system will change by an amount equal to the change in external assets plus the change in local assets; and the change in the liabilities of banking system is equal to the change in the money supply. An excess of gross credit creation over the increase in the money supply over a period must therefore be equivalent to the reduction in the reserves. Not only is this an accounting identity but it is my contention that the absence of such an excess is a reasonably correct criterion for the 'right' rate of monetary expansion in the economies under consideration.

I have been rash enough to incorporate this view into a monograph,[3] which has just emerged from the press, as a recommended 'guide-line' for monetary authorities in this kind of economy. Equilibrium between gross credit creation and the increase in the supply of money is achieved where gross credit creation is equated to that fraction of incremental income given by the incremental ratio between the money supply and income. I have advocated that this should be specified *ex ante* by the central bank publishing a forecast of the target annual increase in the local assets of the banking system to coincide with the annual forecast of income prepared for the budget.

British monetary history is scattered with ineffective attempts to find guide lines for the conduct of monetary policy and no doubt day-to-day management in these rather different economies will continue to be essential; but I believe that some such guide line as this would remove a great deal of misunderstanding about the capacity for inducing growth by monetary creation. The question I would like to end with is whether it is excessively restrictive. I would argue that it is not.

At one extreme the responsible ministers and politicians in these countries are being told that under no circumstances should they indulge in 'deficit finance,' the directors of one of the new East African central banks being presented with a reprint of a lecture by Maurice Frere containing the following:

'This discipline (monetary stability) entails firstly avoidance of any direct or indirect creation of fiduciary money to cover a possible budget deficit'.[4]

At the other extreme greatly exaggerated claims are being made as to the extent to which credit creation can be used to stimulate additional output.

I am in sympathy with the Schumpeter emphasis on the importance of credit creation putting into the right hands the necessary command of resources to facilitate investment; deficit finance is a normal procedure for the private sector. But the dividing line between advocates of deficit finance by government is between those who say it can be done *without* inflation and those who see its operation as being dependent on inflation to secure forced savings. My prescription would be on the conservative side of this line. Its application would allow monetary expansion to take place up to the maximum demanded by the feasible increase in domestic product forecast by the physical planners. It would inevitably 'lead' on the increased output and, to that extent, perform the Schumpeter function and would probably be accompanied by moderate increases in domestic prices. Moreover the limitation on the rate of monetary expansion in my prescription is no more than a recognition of the unavoidable constraint imposed by the effect on the external reserves.

In conclusion it is clear that the analysis in this paper, and the Polak model, will become less and less appropriate as the characteristics are modified by exchange control, import restriction, the growth of domestic money and capital markets combined with non-bank financial institutions and the development of local production of import-substitutes.

Notes and references

1 Polak J.J., 'Monetary Analysis of Income Formation and Payments Problems' *I.M.F. Staff Papers* vol. 6, 1957–58.
  Polak J.J. and Boissonneault L., 'Monetary Analysis of Income and Imports' *I.M.F. Staff Papers* vol. 7, 1959–60.
2 Newlyn, W.T., 'The Supply of Money and its Control' *E.J.* June 1964.
3 Newlyn, W.T. *Finance for Development* (Nairobi 1968).
4 Frere, Maurice *Economic Growth and Monetary Stability* Per Jacobsson Foundation Lecture (Basle 1964).

T. DAVID WILLIAMS

Commodity Distribution in Malawi
A Case Study

The objects of this paper are to describe the location of retail markets for dried fish;[1] to make a preliminary estimate of the relative size of these markets, to indicate the types of trader involved in the distribution of dried fish and to explain the relationship between markets and sources of supply.

The country

Malawi is a relatively long, narrow country, about 500 miles from north to south and about 140 miles wide at its widest point (about 40 miles of this being lake). Approximately one fifth of the total area is lake, much the largest part being Lake Malawi which is 11,430 square miles; Lake Chilwa covers about 1,000 square miles, although about half of this area is marshland. Immediately south of Lake Malawi, and connected to it by a narrow channel is Lake Malombe and the River Shire flows out of Lake Malombe winding in a southerly direction into the lowland area of the Lower Shire and, at the southern tip of Malawi, into Mozambique eventually to become a tributary of the Zambesi. A series of smaller rivers flow in a west to east direction into Lakes Malawi and Chilwa. To the north of Lake Chilwa lies Lake Chiuta which covers up to 440 square miles but has permanent water over only 10 square miles. Lake Chiuta is connected to the larger lake, Amalamba, in Mozambique. Areas around the lakes are relatively lowlying, though the lake surface is about 1500 feet above sea level. About threequarters of the total land area, and the main centres of population, are plateaux between 2,500 and 4,000 feet above sea level.[2]

Lakes Malombe and Chilwa are very shallow and in years of ample rainfall can be, and are, fished intensively by 'semi-traditional' methods in all parts; when rainfall is low a considerable part of both lakes, but especially Chilwa, become mud flats and fishing is severely reduced. Lake Malawi is not only very much deeper but shelves rapidly quite near the shore so that fishing by semi-traditional methods is only possible in a small proportion of the total lake area.

The amount of fish caught in each area varies according to season (some types of fish appearing to have a marked seasonal availability, while others are available throughout the year) and also varies, sometimes dramatically, from one year to another: due, in part, to climatic factors and perhaps also to occasional 'over-fishing' which depletes the stock for succeeding years. It is, therefore, hazardous to estimate the 'normal' catch in a particular area, or even for the country as a whole. The Fisheries Division of the Department of Natural Resources has for several years been recording catches at several of the main fishing areas but until recently they were severely handicapped by shortage of staff; so it is not yet possible to use their data for judging whether there are predictable fluctuations in what appears to have been, until recently, a rising trend in fish production.

The most recent estimate of population is slightly over 4 million and the rate of population increase has recently been very high – probably over 3 per cent a year. This is a predominantly rural population: the Malawi Census gives 4 per cent of the population in urban areas but its definition of an urban area is any place which has in addition to a market and trading stores either a post office or a police post or a works camp. The Census list of 'principal' urban areas includes 7 places with populations of between two and three hundred, the smallest having a population of 203. There are only 5 urban areas in the country with a population over 2,500. The largest, Blantyre-Limbe, is a city with a population of almost 110,000, but this is spread over a considerable area and the population density is less than 1400 per square mile; there are two more urban areas with almost 20,000 population, and the final two – the largest population centres in the Northern Region – have populations of 8,000 and 4,000 respectively.[3]

There are approximately 2,000 miles of 'main road' in the country, but only about 300 miles of these are bituminised.[4] Many principal roads, including the one leading to Salisbury, are very rough under the most favourable circumstances and many others which are quite adequate during the dry season become impassible during the rains and difficult to traverse even after an unseasonal downpour.

The United Transport Company has its own maintenance depots but the private motorist and the 'small' lorry owner would find that in most parts of the country there were no servicing facilities (apart from the provision of petrol and oil). There is a railway line from Chipoka on the south-east of Lake Malawi to Nsanje at the southern tip of the country (and thence to Beira on the Indian Ocean) but the service is a very slow one: the average speed of trains is about twelve miles per hour.[5]

Gross domestic product at factor cost was estimated at £79 million in 1967, of which almost £27 million was due to subsistence production.[6] Per capita income would thus be less than £20 per annum and less than 150,000 Africans are recorded in regular wage employment in Malawi and a substantial proportion of these work on plantations or in domestic service. Less than 15,000 are employed in manufacturing. Moreover the numbers in wage employment as a whole, and in manufacturing, were lower in 1964 than in 1954,[7] though there has probably been a substantial increase since 1964.[8] There are probably more than 150,000 Malawians in wage employment outside the country and remittances from them to Malawi amounted to more than £2 million in 1966.[9]

The growth of fish production

It seems probable that the amount of fish caught at the lake and the amount traded has increased substantially in the last two or three decades as the population has increased – almost doubling since 1945 – and communications have improved. It has, however, already been pointed out that except for the last two or three years, information about total fish production is very unreliable. A report in the mid 1950s, for example, estimated that the total catch at Lake Chilwa was 300 tons a year and that the potential annual catch in the lake was about 1200 tons.[10] In 1966 the recorded catch was approximately 8000 tons.

Some data are available on the catch of the non-African commercial fisheries and though these are probably understatements – with the largest understatement in the early years – they do give some idea of the expansion that has taken place since the 1930s. They cannot be used as indicators of total fish production since a substantial portion of fish taken by 'subsistence' fishermen is probably consumed by the fishermen and their families – an estimate in 1962 was that only 20 per cent of the fish caught by Africans went to the markets.[11] 'Own consumption' is unlikely to have increased much more than the increase in the lake shore population; but the increase in the activities of the commercial firms may reflect the growth in marketing of fish in areas away from the lake shore.

The first permanent non-African fishery was set up by Yiannakis in 1933. By 1937 the estimated annual catch was 29 tons; in 1938 it was 271 tons and despite a setback after the outbreak of war it had risen to 622 tons in 1943. There were by this time other commercial fisheries and the total recorded catch for 1943 was 766 tons. The recorded catch moved up to almost 1300 tons in 1944, went back down to a little over 800 tons in 1945 and back up to 1100 tons in 1946, though the Fisheries Division felt that the latter figure represented a higher proportion of the total real catch than did the earlier figures.[12]

Non-African commercial fishing was concentrated in the southeast arm of Lake Malawi, and by 1958 the recorded catch exceeded 4,300 tons. About 300 tons were caught in the south-west arm.[13] Fears were being expressed that the south-east arm was being over-fished and constraints were placed on the activities of the commercial fisheries; there was apparently local opposition to the commercial companies in the south-west arm and the companies stopped fishing those grounds.

In 1964, when estimates were made of both non-African and African catches in all major areas the reported position was as follows:

TABLE 1   Recorded catches in 1964 (short tons)

	Non-African fisheries	African commercial	African subsistence
S.E.Arm, L.Malawi	2184	287	1704
S.W.Arm, L.Malawi		80	1327
Salima		40	111
Nkhota Kota		84	545
Nkhata Bay		9	72
L.Malombe and Upper Shire		168	1167
L.Chilwa		9	5834

NB 'Commercial' as defined by the Fisheries Division means those fishermen recommended as eligible for special loans from the government.

Source: Appendix X of Annual Report of the Department of Agriculture and Fisheries for the year 1964 Part 1, Government Printer, Zomba, 1965.

Some areas which were not covered at all may have had larger catches than some of the areas which were covered. The other main sources were, and are: Karonga, Deep Bay, Likoma Island, the Lower Shire and Lake Chiuta.

Estimated total catch between 1963 and 1966 is given in table 2.

TABLE 2   Estimated total catch, 1963—1966 (short tons)

year	tons
1963	15,180
1964	14,621 *
1965	20,800
1966	19,300

*This is 1000 tons higher than the figures in 1964 given above.
Source: Compendium of Statistics for Malawi 1966 Table 72.

It is expected that the 1967 figures will be about 15,000, due to a decline in Chilwa from 8,000 to 4,000 tons, and that the Chilwa output will fall to between 1,000 and 2,000 for 1968.[14]

Thus, if one compares the 1939 figures for the non-African fisheries with the 1958 figures, one finds an increase from 200 tons to 4,500 tons, almost all of which was marketed (though not all of it domestically, some of it being exported). If one uses the 1964 figure, after constraints had been put on the commercial fisheries one still finds a tenfold increase over the 1939 figure. If one looks on these figures as an indication of market demand, even if one allows that the early figure was 'too low' both because of under-counting and because there would have been a period during which the fisheries were experimenting with fishing techniques (and thus having an output lower than would be justified by short-run market demand), it would appear reasonable to suggest that demand increased upwards of five-fold.

It is true that the non-African commercial fisheries are engaged mainly in providing fresh fish for a few of the larger population centres – while African traders are mainly dealing in dried fish, both in the larger centre and in the large number of small markets throughout the country, but the factors which would have stimulated demand – population increase, increased income, improved communications – would not have been significant only in the still very small 'larger' centres.

There are no reliable data yet available of the total value of fish production, but a conservative estimate suggests that in 1966 it was at least £1,400,000 which would be about 1·9 per cent of GDP for that year.

The estimate is reached in the following way: (i) assume that total catch was 20,000 tons (this is mainly for computational ease: though it is slightly larger than the official figure, it is probably below the 'real' figure); (ii) assume that 4,000 were from commercial and 16,000 from subsistence fishermen; (iii) assume, in line with footnote 11, that 80 per cent of the catch of subsistence fishermen, and 10 per cent of the catch of commercial fishermen is self consumed: this gives a very conservative figure since a large proportion of the people defined as 'subsistence' fishermen are producing mainly for the market and merely operate on too small a scale to meet the requirement of the 'commercial' category; (iv) assume that all fish is sold 'dried' and that a pound of dried fish equals three pounds of fresh fish: this is also a very conservative assumption since the bulk of the 'non-African' catch and some of the other is sold fresh, at higher prices than those used below for dried fish, and at least some of the dried fish has probably a lower weight loss ratio; (v) assume that

half of the fish that is marketed is sold at major markets and half at
minor markets, though it is almost certain that much more than half
is sold at smaller markets, where the price is higher; (vi) assume
that the retail price of dried fish is 1s. 6d. per pound at lakeshore,
3s. per pound at major markets, and 4s. at smaller markets; these
figures, except perhaps for the lakeshore prices, are almost certainly
very low, but until I have completed analysis of my own extensive
data I would prefer the certainty of erring on the side of conservatism
than the possibility of overstating the value of fish production.

The computations are as follows: of the 4,000 tons from 'commercial' (including non-African) fishermen, 3,600 tons is sold in
markets in the interior; of the 16,000 tons from 'subsistence' fishermen, 3,200 is sold in these markets. Of this 6,800 tons, 3,400 is sold
in major markets; 3,400 tons is sold in smaller markets. In addition
13,200 is self consumed and valued at the opportunity cost of
lakeshore retail prices. 3,400 short tons equals 6,800,000 pounds of
fresh fish, or approximately 2,220,000 pounds of dried fish. 13,200
tons equals 26,400,000 pounds of fresh fish or 8,800 tons of dried
fish.

Thus we have: 2,220,000 pounds at 3s.   6,660,000
2,220,000 pounds at 4s.   8,880,000
8,800,000 pounds at 1s. 6d. 13,200,000
                          _____
                          28,740,000 shillings
which equals £1,437,000

The total GDP in 1966 was £73 million, and £1,400,000 is slightly
over 1·9 per cent of the total.

For the reasons already given, the total real value of fish production is probably substantially higher than that, but it is also very
likely that subsistence production as a whole has been undervalued.

A survey of the consumption patterns of wage and salary earners
in Blantyre-Limbe shows that the lowest income group (under
£5 1s. 8d. per month) devoted 5·6 per cent of their total expenditure
to the purchase of fish. As income increased the percentage spent on
fish decreased. A similar result was reported in an earlier study con-
ducted under the auspices of the Rhodes-Livingstone Institute which,
indeed, found that absolute expenditure on dried fish decreased as
income increased.[15] It would be rash to generalise from these studies
about the percentage of expenditure devoted to fish consumption,
but they do appear to support the 'common-sense' view that dried
fish is the major source of protein for a broad segment of the
population.

Markets and traders

Most markets are under the control of a district or municipal authority. Usually the market area is marked off by a fence or, occasionally, a wall. Most traders, including the fish traders, spread their goods on the ground or on some make-shift table that they have brought with them, but there is often a roofed building which is sometimes walled in, where goods get some protection from the rain or sun. Limbe market is one of the very few in the country where the fish traders always work in an enclosed area. At the other end of the spectrum some markets are simply a group of traders congregated on a grass verge or other space by the roadside.

Markets in the principal urban areas are usually daily markets – with Sundays a closed day in most cases. In other places there will be one, two or three market days (which may include Sunday) each week, always on the same day or days. The markets are not 'closed' on non-market days and often a few fish traders will stay on offering their goods, but there will be few, if any, traders offering other goods, and most fish traders who work in markets that are not daily markets move around from one market to the next to take advantage of the much larger number of customers present on market days.

Neighbouring markets tend, of course, to have different market days. In Chiradzulu district, for example, there are very few daily markets but within the 295 square miles of the district at least three special markets each day of the week (including Sunday) are held.

Traders take their goods to market by lorry, bus, bicycle or in some cases on foot. Lorries regularly call early in the morning at the fishing villages of Southern Lake Malawi and Lake Malcombe and Kachaulu harbour at Lake Chilwa.

Not surprisingly they favour destinations along the 'good' roads and the larger markets can, in any event, be serviced more cheaply: bumping along miles of rough back roads for the sake of one or two traders is neither comfortable nor profitable. The bus company provides passenger service over much of the country, and many traders use the bus service – putting their fish on top of the bus. There are, however, some fishing grounds and some markets which are either inaccessible by bus or accessible only in a markedly inconvenient manner and in these cases the markets are dominated by traders who reach them on bicycle.

Most of the traders are either seasonal or part-time or 'fringe' traders. Seasonal traders are, as the name implies, those who are farmers, or have some other seasonal occupation, and trade during the slack months; part-time traders may visit markets throughout the year but typically confine themselves to one or two short visits of perhaps four or five days each during the month and work on their farms or at some other occupation for the rest of the month; fringe traders are those who would otherwise be unemployed or who are willing to accept a lower income as traders than they could earn as employees because they put a high priority on independence.[16] There are a few fishermen who occasionally take their own fish to market but this is usually because they have been unable to find regular traders at their part of the lake-shore.

There is also a small but significant and, it appears, quite rapidly growing group of what one might call 'entrepreneurial traders'. Perhaps the best way to convey something of the characteristics of this group is to give a brief description of a few traders who talked with the author. *A* left the government service, in which he had held a minor post, in 1954 with savings of £20 and became a trader; in early 1966 he decided to buy a boat and nets and employ some fishermen; by late 1967 he had bought three boats, all equipped with outboard motors – these and the nets would have a capital value of between £300 and £500 – and was employing about 30 men either for fishing or maintenance work as well as continuing trading activities. *B* started as a fisherman; he saved enough to buy a boat and nets, at first assisted by relatives, then gradually acquired several boats and became an employer; he began to take his fish to markets instead of selling it at the lakeshore and now markets his fish as far away as Rhodesia. *C* had been a domestic servant and saved £15 or £20 and became a trader; about ten years later he was clearing three to four hundred pounds a year (which was about five times what he would have made if he had remained a domestic servant).

None of these people (and there are several more cases which could be cited but they would show a similar pattern) have yet achieved a degree of affluence which would, by the standards of 'developed' economies – even if one makes a generous allowance for the differences between comparative money income and comparative real income – take them out of the ranks of very small businessmen. But not only have they achieved a level of affluence which is substantial in terms of the income levels prevailing in Malawi but they have been able first to save ten or twenty pounds out of a very meagre income, and then with nothing to help them except their intelligence and a willingness to work hard, have been able in a few years to increase their income fivefold or more.

This group seems to have emerged within the last ten to fifteen years, though there may have been occasional examples earlier. It is likely that there will be increasing numbers of 'entrepreneurs' in the next decade, but whether many of them will be able to make the additional progress that would see them established as business-proprietors remains to be seen.

An accumulation of about £20 of capital, from whatever source, appears to be a critical factor in the emergence of the 'entrepreneur'. To understand why this is so, it is necessary to say something about the structure of distribution. There are up to four distinct stages in the distributive process, though two or three of them may be handled by the same trader. First, the fish is dried (either by smoking, sun-drying or a combination) and then may be sold at the lakeshore; second, it may be transported to one of the larger markets and then sold wholesale; third, it may be retailed at one of the larger markets or sold at 'semi-wholesale' either to one of the smaller traders in the large market (who has found it difficult to buy from the main wholesalers because they are interested in people buying larger quantities) or to small traders who will, fourth, retail at the lesser markets.

There is a certain amount of vertical integration: some traders cover the first three steps, buying fresh fish, drying it, taking it to a major market and retailing it themselves; in most areas the first two stages are carried out by the same trader and it is only in a few places that there is a distinctive group which buys fresh fish, dries it and then sells it to traders at the lakeshore. There are also some traders who buy fresh fish at the lake and, after drying it, take it directly to the minor markets, but these are almost always 'bicycle traders'; those who frequent the markets that are difficult to reach by lorry or bus.

The difference between the dried fish price at lakeshore and the retail price at a major market is typically about $1 : 2\frac{1}{2}$. The traders' costs include transportation and the opportunity-cost of time spent buying fish from lakeshore dealers – which if there is a shortage of fish or if the trader has not established contacts – may be two or three weeks or even more. If the trader buys fresh fish and dries it himself, it will usually take about three days after he acquired the fish to dry it properly and he will have to rent a drying rack, buy firewood and perhaps employ helpers.

For the astute trader potential profits are better than that usually obtained by retailing, but overheads are relatively high: in a country where the per capita cash income is about £10 per year, 'overheads' of three or four pounds are significant. There is also a greater risk element in buying at lakeshore. The trader who buys at, or near, the market at which he intends to sell knows the balance between supply and demand that existed in that market the previous day; the man who has spent a week or two at the lakeshore may misjudge the tide. True, he can move elsewhere – but that not only involves additional transport costs but another guess about the balance in a different market. So, in addition to predictable overheads, a man must be prepared to take a loss. A 'capital' of about £20 is often considered a necessary starting sum.

Numbers and size of markets

This paper deals with markets visited by the author or his assistants. Districts close to Chancellor College (in Limbe) were covered most intensively. It is unlikely that many markets, except very small ones, were entirely missed in the Southern Region. Three districts in the Central and Northern Regions had to be excluded completely, but none of them are as significant, in terms of market activity, as most of those that were covered. Most of the markets in the Central and Northern Regions were visited but these visits took place, almost entirely, during the university's long vacation from July to early October.

The breadth of coverage does, however, raise some problems. The 'average size' of markets has been estimated in terms of the average number of traders recorded on visits to the market, multiplied by the number of market days, the total supplemented by an estimate of the numbers trading on non-market days, and the total divided by six to give 'average per week-day'.

Several markets were visited infrequently (some only once) and it is difficult to know to what extent the reported numbers are 'typical'. Apart from distinctions between market and non-market days, there are seasonal, monthly and other variations in market activity. One may indeed find significant proportional variations during the course of a day. Wherever possible, an attempt was made to get information from traders, market supervisors and local people. All 'large' markets were visited several times – the most frequently visited being Limbe (one of the two largest in the country) for which there are almost 100 recorded visits.

It is, however, possible that the significance of some markets were either under- or over-estimated to the extent that the real average might be double or half the recorded average. It is most unlikely that any of the 20 largest markets was significantly underrated. On the other hand, it is quite possible that the numbers of small markets has been underestimated by 20 to 30 per cent.

There has only been one other attempt to get information about the activities of fish traders throughout the country. In 1964 the Government asked district councils to submit information about the average number of fishtraders in markets controlled by the districts. Several districts apparently did not submit returns; most of the larger markets do not come under district authority, and there are many 'small' markets which are entirely independent. One has no way of evaluating the accuracy of their returns. However, for districts in which the author's survey and the district returns covered a reasonably large number of the same markets, the total number of traders for these markets was close. There were a few instances where individual markets gave markedly different results but these may have been due to real changes in fish production from various sources (in brief: the 1964 figures were higher for markets mainly served by Lake Chilwa and lower for Central Region markets served by Lake Malawi and where the author's estimate may, in any event, be too high because of the timing of his survey of that region).

It appears to be the case that the Central and Northern Regions markets are a great deal more active during the July-October period than during (for example) November-March. This is because this is an 'off-season' for farmers who turn to trading and because there is more cash available at this time after the harvesting of crops than there would be in the growing season. The Southern Region having a much higher proportion of wage earners would be less susceptible to the effects of 'harvest-income'. Hearsay and a very limited number of direct investigations, suggest that markets in most districts of the Central and Northern Regions have only half as many traders – or less – during the November–April period as they have during the July–October period. Most markets in the Southern Region appear to have a steady level of activity except perhaps for an upsurge around Christmas and the New Year.

Table 3, below, shows the distribution of markets by size. The cumulative significance of 'small' markets compared with (relatively)

TABLE 3 Average number of fish traders per day at Malawi markets recorded by the author

Number of traders	Number of markets
40 and over	2
29–34	5
22–26	7
15–19	6
13	4
12	7
11	2
10	8
9	4
8	10
7	14
6	18
5	12
4	26
3	17
2	21
1	22

'large' markets is not perhaps unusual. The very small scale of the 'small' markets is, however, significant if one considers suggestions for improving the system of distribution by introducing more 'efficient' or more 'modern' methods. To present a full picture of the situation would require estimates of the value of fish sold in markets. Data have been collected and are being analysed. Details cannot yet be given but for the purposes of this paper, one may assume that the average retail value of fish sold per trader per day is between £1 and £1 10s. There are a few traders who have a much higher turnover, and many who have a slightly lower one, but these variations are not crucial to the present discussion.

One half of all traders are in markets with ten traders or less; more than one quarter are in markets with six traders or less. Almost half of all markets have four traders or less.

Average daily turnover is higher in the large markets but, on the other hand, there are two factors which indicate that the relative significance of large markets is greatly overestimated by table 3. First, fifteen of the twenty largest markets were in the Central and Northern Regions and were visited during their peak activity. Second, our twenty to thirty per cent estimate of 'missed' markets would almost all (perhaps all) come in the smaller group – four or five traders at most.

Intensity of trading (the ratio of traders to population) appears to be closely related to population density. In order to examine this, we have compared the number of traders per district to the population of the district.

There are, of course, many markets which lie near the border of a district and it is not proper to assume that all customers come from the district in which the market is situated. This problem would, however, arise no matter what geographical area was used and it seems not unreasonable to suppose that the effects of 'border markets' cancel out. It is also likely that larger markets will attract some outside customers who make a special trip to take advantage of the wider range of offerings. But because of the rather rudimentary transport facilities, a trip of twenty or thirty miles becomes something of an expedition, quite possibly involving an overnight stop if one wants to stay at the destination for two or three hours.

In the following table trader and population density for the Southern Region is given by district except for Blantyre. The exception is due not only to the fact that Blantyre is much the largest urban area in the country, but to the fact that Blantyre District includes a very large, sparsely populated area with few fish markets: the totals for Blantyre District would, consequently, be affected by two radically divergent influences.

TABLE 4   Trading intensity and population density, Southern Region

	Average no. of traders[1]	Population[2]	Intensity (rounded)	Population density[2] (pop. per sq. mile)
Blantyre Urban	114	109,795	1−960	1393
Chiradzulu	113	141,870	1−1,260	481
Cholo	138	245,508	1−1,780	381
Zomba	140	281,806	1−2,010	284
Nsanje	47	101,074	1−2,150	135
Blantyre District (exc. Bl. Urban)	66	170,025	1−2,580	
Mlanje	120	398,762	1−3,320	300
Kasupe	58	225,422	1−3,890	98
Fort Johnston	36[3]	231,827	1−6,440	96
Chikwawa	15	157,805	1−10,520	83

Notes

[1] The average number of traders is based entirely on recorded visits to markets except for Zomba, Mlanje and Chikwawa. For these three districts there were district markets, for which figures were given in 1964, which we had not covered. Estimates for these markets were included on the assumption that the relation between 1964 and 1967 figures for these markets would be the same as that for markets which were covered on both occasions. The 1964 data did not, however, include markets not controlled by the District Council. Because of the large number of tea estates in Cholo and Mlanje, which have markets that are not controlled by the District Councils, it is probable that these districts suffer from the greatest degree of under-representation.

[2] Population and Population Density are from Table V, *Provisional Report, Malawi Population Census 1966.*

[3] Fort Johnston District is the centre of the commercial fisheries. Most of their fish is taken to the principal urban areas but some is sold locally. It is sold fresh, and thus lies outside the scope of this paper but it is possible that in their absence there would be a large local market — as there is in Salima and Nkhota Kota — which would include some dried-fish traders.

Data on the Central and Northern Region markets show a rather uneven relationship between 'intensity' and 'density', but coverage of these markets, as already explained, was confined to a short period of the year, and the short time available for coverage of so large an area makes it likely that in some districts there were a large number of markets missed altogether. This was certainly the case in Dedza, and the figures given below not only underestimate the amount of trading in Dedza but underestimate its relative amount. Another problem is that the average value per trader not only varies considerably among markets, as it does in the south, but it appears to be the case that the average turnover in some markets with a large number of traders is considerably less than in some markets with fewer traders. This occasionally occurs in the south, but there 'number of traders' appears to be more closely related to 'total sales'.

TABLE 5   Trading intensity and population density,
Central and Northern Regions[1]

	Average no. of traders	Population	Intensity	Density
Dowa	107	181,178	1−1,690	150
Lilongwe	251	499,730	1−1,990	381
Salima[2]	37	85,046	1−2,300	111
Nkhota Kota[2]	26	62,961	1−2,420	38
Ntchisi	25	66,612	1−2,670	104
Rumpi[2]	12	46,619	1−2,970	25
Ncheu	45	164,107	1−3,648	124
Nkhata Bay	20	83,898	1−4,190	53
Mzimba	54	229,900	1−4,260	57
Kasungu	16	98,154	1−6,330	33
Dedza[3]	20	229,884	1−11,490	165

Notes
[1] Three districts − Karonga, Chitipa and Mchinje were not covered at all.
[2] Almost the entire district number were found at the principal town.
[3] Dedza, as mentioned above, had much the poorest coverage of all districts included in tables 4 and 5.

The road system is less adequate in the Central and Northern Regions than in the south, particularly with respect to feeder roads, so it is not perhaps surprising that population density is not so closely related with numbers of traders.

What is surprising about the data is that of the twelve areas with the greatest intensity, six of them are in the Central and Northern Regions. It is, however, quite likely that if data were obtained for the entire year, there would be a considerable drop, with Lilongwe, Ncheu and Dedza showing the greatest consistency.

Relation between source and market

For much of the period during which we were studying the markets, there was an unusually low output of fish from Lake Chilwa. Those markets in the Southern Region where Chilwa fish is usually a dominant or substantial proportion of total sales were covered quite well before the effects of the lake-fall radically changed the situation. But markets further afield where Chilwa fish might normally have been a significant minority group had almost no Chilwa fish during our survey. In December 1966, for example, Chilwa fish was being sold in Lilongwe and in Fort Jameson, across the Zambian border. Surveys undertaken by Mr Renson of the Fisheries Department, show that Chilwa fish was consistently reaching Lilongwe during 1966. Our reports for July–October 1967 and December 1967–January 1968 record less than one per cent of traders in Lilongwe market who had got their fish from Chilwa.

Map 3 shows the source of fish for all markets in each district of the Southern Region before the effects of the lake-fall. There is obviously a very close relationship between source and geographical distance, but the greater significance of Lake Malawi fish in Cholo than Chiradzulu cannot be explained in these terms.

Principal Cholo markets are more accessible to traders from Lake Malawi since they are situated along the bituminised main road, while most Chiradzulu markets lie off the main road and are reached by rather rough feeder roads. Moreover, since the Chiradzulu markets are not daily markets most traders move each day to a new market, and the bus service is not very convenient for this purpose. Chiradzulu, like Mlanje, is normally served by traders who travel by bicycle from Lake Chilwa. Traders from the Lower Shire tend to follow the railway, both because the railway runs through Nsanje and Chiromo and because the principal road between Chiromo and Cholo is effectively closed for some months of the year. One finds a spur of Lower Shire traders jutting into the Chilwa-Malawi areas. Map 4 shows the larger markets and their sources in relation to the main road and railway system.

When the waters of Chilwa receded, there was a substantial flow of Lake Malawi fish into Chiradzulu and even into Mlanje. There was also a considerable increase in the number of traders who were bringing fish from Lake Chiuta and from Lake Amalamba in Mozambique. This was the case not only in Chiradzulu and Mlanje but also (to a lesser extent) in Zomba and Blantyre. It also appears to be the case (though there is less comparative data on this) that traders were coming from further north than usual on Lake Malawi – from Salima, Nkhota Kota and even further north. The very limited recent data from Lilongwe, the major fish market outside the Southern Region (and perhaps the major single market in the country) suggest that very little fish from the southern part of Lake Malawi has been going there – presumably because it is flowing into the Southern Region to fill the vacuum created by the absence of Chilwa fish – and while there are still a large number of traders in

Lilongwe market they come almost exclusively from Salima and fishing grounds further north.

There are probably some Southern Region markets where the volume of fish trading fell off in 1967, but the almost complete drying-up of the major source for many areas did not lead to the catastrophic imbalance that would have occurred if the distributive system had been an inefficient one relying on tradition-bound or 'lazy' traders. Sensitivity to new opportunities was keen, and traders responded quickly.

There is not enough data to indicate whether the shift in the movement of traders was prompted by opportunities for higher prices or more rapid turnover. Whatever the traders' motives, the consumers suffered remarkably little inconvenience when the usual source of fish for the area almost completely dried up.

Summary and conclusions

Per capita income is low in Malawi; the population is almost entirely rural, and only a small part of the country is served by good all weather roads. Almost all parts of the country are, however, reasonably close to lakes or rivers which provide edible fish.

Fish marketing has increased substantially since the second world war; most markets are, however, very small, and most traders accept low returns because there are few alternative means of getting, or supplementing, an income.

There is a small, but increasing, number of traders who operate on a larger scale and who have many of the characteristics of an actual, or incipient, entrepreneurial group.

Despite the unorganised structure of distribution the pattern that has emerged corresponds closely to the pattern that 'should' be present in a well organised economic system. Wholesale and retail functions are sensitive to a variety of specific needs; the densest population areas, even though they may have few, or no, urban centres, attract the greatest number of traders; traders usually move to markets which are most accessible, but there is a rapid adjustment in 'usual' patterns when markets cannot be supplied in their 'usual' manner.

Acknowledgments
Research for this paper was assisted by financial help from the Lake Chilwa Project of the University of Malawi, supported by a Leverhulme grant. The Project financed the employment of research assistants, including several students who worked during vacations. I am especially indebted to C.A.L.Bai, who was a full-time research assistant before entering the university as a student.

I am also grateful to H. Renson and R. Kirk of the (then) Ministry of
Natural Resources at Zomba, who were always willing to share their
experience and enthusiasm. Ray Harris of the Department of Geography at
Edinburgh University helped to prepare the maps.
The paper has been amplified at some points as a result of discussion at
the Conference.

Notes and references

1 Fresh fish is largely confined to the lakeshore and a small number of the
biggest markets. It is usually taken to major centres by non-African firms
which have insulated trucks and access to cold storage facilities, and is
then sold wholesale to African traders. Even in the biggest markets the
number of traders dealing in dried fish is much larger than the number
dealing in fresh fish, and in most markets throughout the country the
volume of dried fish sales is many times greater than the volume of fresh
fish sales.
2 J. G. Pike and G. T. Rimmington *Malawi: A Geographical Study* (Oxford
1965) *passim.*
3 *Malawi Population Census* 1966: *Provisional Report.*
4 In June 1966 there were 1759 miles of main road, of which 236 were
bituminised. *Compendium of Statistics for Malawi* 1966 table 104.
5 *Compendium,* table 96.
6 *Economic Report* 1967 Ministry of Economic Affairs.
7 *Compendium,* table 8. Numbers rose to 1960 (1961 for manufacturing) and
fell substantially afterwards.
8 *Economic Report* 1967 p.28.
9 *Compendium* table 17.
10 *Report of the Inquiry into the Fishing Industry* (Zomba 1957) paragraph 6.
11 The estimate was that 'up to 80 per cent' of the catch of subsistence
fishermen, and 'between 5 and 20 per cent' caught by African commercial
fisherman went to own consumption. *Fisheries Development Possibilities in
Nyasaland* F.A.O. No. 1761, Rome, 1963.
12 *Report on the Tilapia and Other Fish and Fisheries of Lake Nyasa,*
(London 1952) pp. 42–45.
13 *Annual Report of the Department of Agriculture and Fisheries*
14 *Economic Report* 1967 p. 26.
15 *Blantyre/Limbe Income-Expenditure Surveys (BLIS) August,* 1965
December 1965 and *April* 1966 Government Press, Zomba and *Patterns of
Income and Expenditure, Blantyre/Limbe, Nyasaland* by D. G. Bettison and
P. J. Rigby (Rhodes-Livingstone Institute 1961).
16 On one occasion I met a 'subsistence' trader. He had been a trader for
over thirty years, often carrying small amounts very long distances. His
meagre return was just about enough to meet the additional cost of food
and accommodation incurred in being away from home. He had apparently
never made more than this, and seemed quite resigned about it.

Maps overleaf.

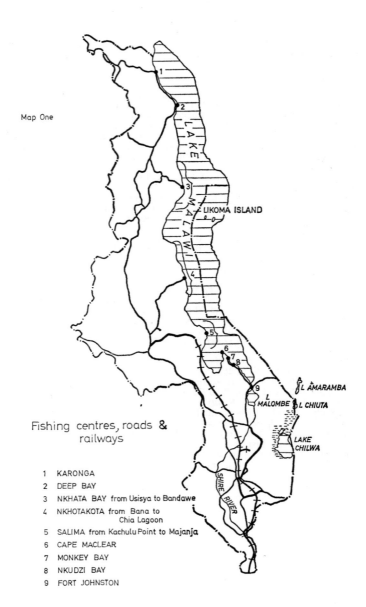

Map One

LAKE MALAWI

LIKOMA ISLAND

L AMARAMBA

L MALOMBE   L CHIUTA

LAKE CHILWA

SHIRE RIVER

Fishing centres, roads &
railways

1   KARONGA
2   DEEP BAY
3   NKHATA BAY from Usisya to Bandawe
4   NKHOTAKOTA from Bana to
                    Chia Lagoon
5   SALIMA from Kachulu Point to Majanja
6   CAPE MACLEAR
7   MONKEY BAY
8   NKUDZI BAY
9   FORT JOHNSTON

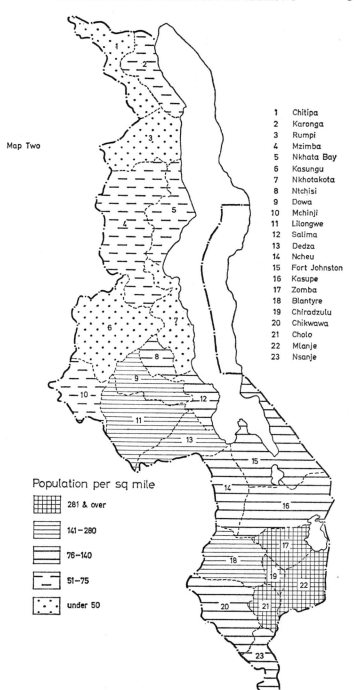

Map Two

1   Chitipa
2   Karonga
3   Rumpi
4   Mzimba
5   Nkhata Bay
6   Kasungu
7   Nkhotakota
8   Ntchisi
9   Dowa
10 Mchinji
11 Lilongwe
12 Salima
13 Dedza
14 Ncheu
15 Fort Johnston
16 Kasupe
17 Zomba
18 Blantyre
19 Chiradzulu
20 Chikwawa
21 Cholo
22 Mlanje
23 Nsanje

Population per sq mile

281 & over

141 – 280

76 – 140

51 – 75

under 50

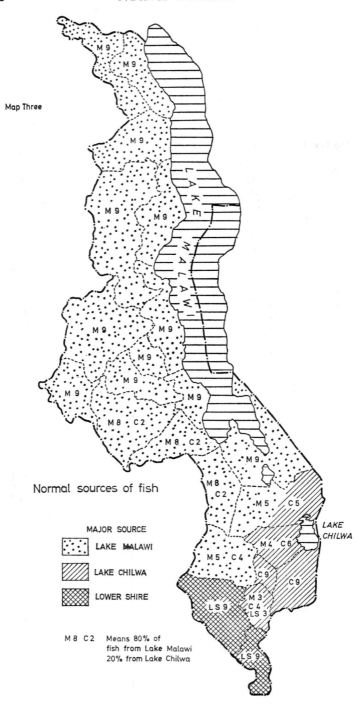

Map Three

Normal sources of fish

MAJOR SOURCE

LAKE MALAWI

LAKE CHILWA

LOWER SHIRE

M 8   C 2   Means 80% of
fish from Lake Malawi
20% from Lake Chilwa

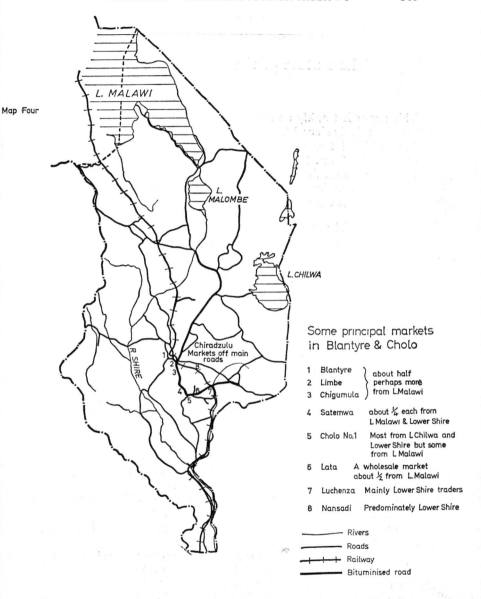

Map Four

Some principal markets
in Blantyre & Cholo

1 Blantyre ⎫ about half
2 Limbe   ⎬ perhaps more
3 Chigumula ⎭ from L.Malawi

4 Satemwa   about ¼ each from
           L Malawi & Lower Shire

5 Cholo No.1 Most from L Chilwa and
              Lower Shire but some
              from L Malawi

6 Lata   A wholesale market
          about ½ from L.Malawi

7 Luchenza Mainly Lower Shire traders

8 Nansadi   Predominately Lower Shire

——————— Rivers
————————— Roads
++++++ Railway
———————— Bituminised road

W.B.REDDAWAY

The Future of the Ghanaian Economy

This paper is frankly an attempt to examine a belief which I have
held intuitively since I first became concerned with Ghanaian affairs
(and which I find to be widely shared), and to do it in a semi-
quantitative form. Fundamentally, my object is to examine how far
the basic restoration of the Ghanaian balance of payments – and
with it the creation of a truly viable economy – depends on a large
increase in the output of agriculture, other than cocoa.

Statement of the problem

In qualitative terms, the problem may be posed in the following way:
  (*a*) In 1967 Ghana will have balanced her external payments
  with the help of many abnormal factors: (i) borrowing from
  the IMF; (ii) special loans and grants from other countries;
  (iii) a major postponement of debt payments; (iv) substantial
  imports of goods on suppliers' credits, arranged before the coup;
  (v) a subnormal level of aggregate demand, enforced partly by
  a deflationary policy and partly by import controls on materials,
  which forcibly limited the earning of incomes; (vi) a policy of
  import restriction, which forced consumers and investors to
  devote an artificially low proportion of their aggregate demand
  to imports; (vii) restrictions on remittances of profits.
  (*b*) Many of the above items cannot be used in future years,
  and some call for *reverse* effects: the IMF must be repaid,
  interest and amortisation grow with the increase in debt, etc.
  (*c*) As output expands, demand for goods of a type now
  imported will grow, and indeed grow markedly (machinery,
  imported materials, consumer durables).
  (*d*) There are some favourable factors, such as higher production
  of manufactures or semi-manufactures which are now imported;
  but it seems inevitable that imports of non-agricultural products
  will grow substantially.
  (*e*) This means that there are only 3 important ways in which
  the balance of payments can be improved: (i) there should be
  a (gross) inflow of capital to cover 'bankable' or commercial
  projects; (ii) there should be an increase in exports of manufactures or services; (iii) there must be a big increase in the output
  of agricultural products, which must be sufficient to produce

an increased proportion of Ghana's food (despite the large rise in total consumption), meet a good part of the increased need for raw materials (cotton, sugar cane, tobacco) and produce a larger surplus which can be profitably sold abroad.

(*f*) The absolute amount which can be expected from (i) and (ii) in the last point is rather limited; the scope for increasing cocoa exports is in practice limited by market considerations; hence the need for rather radical action on the production of other agricultural products.

The problem then is to try to put some reasonable numbers on all this. To do it properly would require both much more information and much more time than I possess, but it seems worth while to explore the orders of magnitude. One is inevitably concerned with *production* as well as trade, and it has to be divided in some degree of types.

The world bank model

For the purpose of this exercise I rely heavily on the 'demonstration model' included in the World Bank report for 14 March 1967. The relevant characteristics of this model are:

(*a*) It assumed a growth of gross domestic product after 1968 at 4·5 per cent a year.

(*b*) As one of the conditions for securing this, the ratio of investment to GDP is assumed to rise from 12·3 per cent in 1969 to 13·3 per cent in 1975.

(*c*) The average domestic savings ratio is assumed to be 8 per cent in 1968, and the marginal domestic savings rate is assumed to be 25 per cent.

(*d*) It is assumed that exports of goods will increase by 4·4 per cent a year.

(*e*) All measurements from 1968 onwards are made at constant prices.

All the above assumptions relate to what is produced, consumed or traded in Ghana (but say nothing about payments of interest, 'aid' or external financing matters generally). They therefore imply, as a matter of arithmetic, a movement in Ghana's figures for merchandise imports which comes out as a rise of 1·6 per cent a year, starting from £151 million in 1968.[1]

The external financial accounts which might accompany the Bank's model are then presented in two possible forms (out of many possible ones), one of which assumed that the financial deficits in the various years are largely met by loans on concessional terms, the other assuming normal terms.

The Bank's model was designed primarily for the special purpose of showing the effects of different schemes of financing, and correspondingly treats various items in unconventional ways (see *World Bank Report*, p. 104): the 'deficit on goods and services' includes income payable abroad on pre-1966 investments, but not income payable on subsequent private and public investments (which are subtracted respectively from private and public investment). Rewriting the 1975 figures in more conventional form, and taking the concessional terms assumption, the figures are as in table 1.

TABLE 1   Capital account in 1975

Requirements	£ million	Met by	£ million
Deficit on goods and services	44	Gross private investment	13
Repayment of suppliers credits	13	Grants and food loans	10
Repayment of long-term debt	5	Other gross public investment	39
Total	62		62

Note: The bank figures have been converted from Cedis to £s at the old rate of exchange.

This table is mentioned to show that, even if the intervening deficits are financed on concessional terms, the final balance of payments position is one which requires some optimism about future capital inflows: in practice, the structural adjustments needed will probably have to be more drastic than the Bank assumes, in order that the external financial position should be easier.

Statistical approximations for 1965

In order to consider this sort of problem properly, one ought to have a full-scale input-output model of the economy. This exercise is no more than a pioneer attempt to show how the position might look, using pure assumptions for many of the initial breakdowns: given the changes in the various aggregates shown by the World Bank model, one can see something of the *adjustments* which are needed in the more detailed figures.

First, we attempted some basic tables for 1965. All these should be repeated with more care, preferably for a less abnormal year (e.g., 1966); the various devices used in arriving at the figures do not justify a description, apart from a few notes in the appendix.

(*a*) Table 2 breaks down the value of the gross domestic product at market prices for 1965 between six industries, adds the value of the inputs (including those bought from other enterprises in the same sector) and so gives the gross value of the output. The definition of the sectors is in some respects a compromise between what seemed to be (approximately) available, and what would be most useful.

(b) Table 3 takes production for each industry, adds on imports, and shows a rough allocation of the total supply between usage as an input item for further economic activity and figures for each of the final uses, including export.
It should be emphasized that the products of 'manufacturing' include many semi-manufactures, such as steel or cement.

TABLE 2   Analysis of gross domestic product at market prices, 1965

Type of activity	Gross value added	Materials used	Value of output
		Million (old) Cedis	
Agriculture, forestry, fishing (including cocoa marketing and food processing)	950	67*	1,017*
Mining and quarrying	42	13	55
Manufacturing (including power and water)	170	150	320
Construction (excluding repair work)	116	94	210
Transport and trade	290	65*	355*
Services (including government services)	340	40	380
Total gross domestic product	1,908	429	2,337

*Goods brought for sale are not included either as materials or as value of output.

Calculating the 'standard' position for 1975

For 1975 we sought to produce corresponding tables (4 and 5), taking the control figures in the World Bank report for gross domestic product and for each type of final usage.[2] Some further information had to be supplied, and this section describes our 'standard' case. (Whatever assumptions one makes, the World Bank figure for *total* imports necessarily emerges.)

The main assumptions used were as follows:
(a) The analysis of exports given by the World Bank was used. (Later on, we express doubts about its *total size*).
(b) The totals for each kind of internal final usage were allocated between types of goods in roughly the 1965 proportions, but with some increase in the percentage of personal consumption going to manufactures.

TABLE 3   Balance of the economy, 1965

Million (old) Cedis

| Item | Goods and services of a kind produced by: | | | | | | |
	Agri-culture, etc.	Min-ing	Manu-factur-ing, etc.	Con-struc-tion	Trans-port and trade	Ser-vices	Total
Supply							
Production in Ghana	1,017	55	320	210	355	380	2,337
Imports (c.i.f.)	49	11	344	—	17	33	454
Total supply	1,066	66	664	210	372	413	2,791
Usage							
Current inputs into:							
1. Agriculture, etc.	25	—	20	—	20	2	67
2. Mining	—	—	10	—	3	—	13
3. Manufacturing, etc.	10	10	115	—	10	5	150
4. Construction	10	3	65	—	11	5	94
5. Transport and trade	—	—	50	—	10	5	65
6. Services	6	—	20	—	7	7	40
Total current inputs	51	13	280	—	61	24	429
Exports (including re-exports)	215	52	7	—	18	8	300
Personal consumption	789	—	240	—	276	201	1,506
Government consumption	10	1	42	1	12	180	246
Investments	1	—	95	209	5	—	310
Total usage	1,066	66	664	210	372	413	2,791

TABLE 4   Analysis of gross domestic product at market prices, 1975

Million (old) Cedis

Type of activity	Gross value added	Materials used	Value of output	Percentage increase on 1965
Agriculture, etc.	1,343	95	1,438	41
Mining and quarrying	56	17	73	33
Manufacturing, etc.	340	300	640	100
Construction	137	112	249	19
Transport and trade	397	89	486	37
Services (including government)	480	56	536	42
Total gross domestic product	2,753	669	3,422	44

TABLE 5   Balance of the economy, 1975

Million (old) Cedis

Item	Goods and services of a kind produced by:						
	Agricul-ture, etc.	Min-ing	Manu-factur-ing, etc.	Con-struc-tion	Trans-port and trade	Ser-vices	Total
Supply							
Production in Ghana	1,438	73	640	249	486	536	3,422
Imports (c.i.f.)	44	21	334	—	24	48	471
Total supply	1,482	94	974	249	510	584	3,893
Usage							
Current inputs into :							
1. Agriculture, etc.	36	—	28	—	28	3	95
2. Mining	—	—	13	—	4	—	17
3. Manufacturing, etc.	20	20	230	—	20	10	300
4. Construction	12	4	77	—	13	6	112
5. Transport and trade	—	—	68	—	14	7	89
6. Services	8	—	28	—	10	10	56
Total current inputs	76	24	444	—	89	36	669
Exports (including re-exports)	330	—	10	—	20	18	447
Personal consump-tion	1,060	69	350	—	378	275	2,063
Government con-sumption	14	—	60	1	17	255	348
Investment	2	1	110	248	6	—	366
Total usage	1,482	94	974	249	510	584	3,893

(c) For four of the six columns – trade and transport, other services, construction and mining – the part of the total supplies which goes to inputs is relatively small, and so is the amount of imports, so that the whole column of table 5 was virtually determined by the amounts going to final usage.[3]

(d) Assuming the same ratio of input to output in each industry, this gives the gross domestic product and 'materials used' for four of the six industries in table 4.

(e) The total of GDP in table 4 left a figure for agriculture and manufacturing combined of 1,683 million (old) Cedis, a rise of just over 50 per cent compared with 1965. For the 'standard'

case it was assumed that the output of manufacturing would
have doubled, leaving agriculture with a rise of 41 per cent.
(The implications of other assumptions are discussed below).
Assuming again the same input-output ratio, this enabled
table 4 to be completed.

(f) The total inputs into each industry were then transferred
to table 5, and split along the rows in the 1965 proportions.

(g) This gave the imports of agricultural products and of
manufactures, and the total of the imports duly added to the
World Bank figure.

Conclusions with the standard case

The interesting conclusions arise essentially in the fields of agriculture
and manufacturing.

1. *Agriculture.* Taking the figures as they stand, the implications
for agriculture are:

(a) Total output has to be increased by 41 per cent in ten
years – a formidable task, but certainly not impossible when
there is a lot of under-utilised land.

(b) The export figure has increased by 53 per cent, the details
being as in table 6, in million old Cedis.

TABLE 6   Exports of agricultural products

			Million (old) Cedis
	1965	*1975*	*% Increase*
Cocoa and products	179	271	51
Timber	32	50	56
Other	4	9	125
Total	215	330	53

The World Bank is assuming that producers of the first two
will be able to increase both production and sales of these
(largely export) industries in this way, which would certainly have
been very optimistic for timber in the absence of devaluation. The
final item includes their estimates of the rubber which will be
available for export; the figure remains extremely small.

(c) Imports are shown as falling by 10 per cent below the 1965
level, although the import figure has to cover imports of
things not produced (or hardly produced) in Ghana, such as
wheat and some fancy European foodstuffs. Seeing that the
imports in 1965 were at a low level and that the total population
will have increased, it seems likely that this implies a substantial
increase in the output of 'difficult' items to keep the total
import so low.

(*d*) A product-by-product analysis would be needed to see whether such a low figure for imports really makes sense – or rather, to see whether it would be easier for agriculture to produce the same effective result by increasing its general exports (excluding cocoa and timber) than by attempting so much import substitution. It would in any case be highly desirable to increase these exports, as an insurance against failure to achieve the Bank's targets for cocoa and timber: this involves both a production effort and a sales effort (e.g. on fish, bananas or maize).

2. *Manufacturing*. In the case of manufacturing the problem is essentially one of *composition*, for which again a much more detailed analysis is really needed. As they stand, the figures in table 7 give the following picture, covering semi-manufactures as well as finished goods.

TABLE 7   Supply of manufactures for home or export use

			Million (old) Cedis
	1965	*1975*	*Change*
Produced in Ghana	320	640	+320
Imported	344	334	−10
Total	664	974	+310
Of which semi-manufactures for use in Ghana	280	444	+164

This seems to me to have an improbable look about it, seeing that exports are negligible (only 10 million Cedis in 1975). It does not seem likely that the usage of semi-manufactures could very substantially exceed the total figure for imported manufactures – which must itself include a great deal of machinery.

Since the method of approach is really concerned with the figure for net imports (i.e. imports less exports) it would be formally possible to realise a 'solution' which did not look outside the column for manufacturing: one might assume the same volume of production but with much more going to export and much more imported. The problem with this – even given an Economic Community for West Africa – is to have any faith in exports reaching an adequate scale.

3. *Tentative conclusion:* If the GDP and its internal uses are taken as given, it seems that a more plausible position would emerge if the economy were made more export-oriented; this could be done by having a rather greater increase in the output and exports of agricultural products, and rather more imports of manufactured products

in exchange – or else by securing a break-through in the export of manufactures. All these possibilities, however, clearly raise structural problems of a formidable nature, which can not be solved simply by monetary or fiscal means related to saving, etc.

In so far as it might well be necessary to increase exports relatively to imports, in order that the 'financial' problem set out in table 1 might be ameliorated, the best hope would be by raising exports. (There would of course then have to be a reduction in internal usage, if the GDP were held constant).

An alternative case

The possibility sketched in the last section may be illustrated by assuming that the value added in agriculture was raised by 50 million Cedis above the standard assumption (giving an increase on 1965 of 47 per cent) and that of manufacturing correspondingly reduced by 50 million Cedis (giving an increase on 1965 of 70 per cent).

So far as agriculture is concerned, this would, with the extra materials, mean an increase in output of 54 million Cedis. If the old figures for exports were maintained, this would result in a negative figure for imports, which is clearly impossible: instead, we might visualise the whole increase in supply as going to exports.

In the case of manufacturing, the reduction in output would be 94 million Cedis, but a large part of the fall in inputs would themselves be manufactures. If we leave the exports unchanged, and allow for minor consequential effects working through other columns, the new position for agriculture and manufacturing would come out roughly as in table 8.

TABLE 8   Alternative possibilities for agriculture and manufacture

	Agriculture			Manufacturing		Million (old) Cedis
	1975 Standard case	1975 Alterna- tive	1965	1975 Standard case	1975 Alterna- tive	1965
Supply						
Production	1,438	1,492	1,017	640	546	320
Imports	44	44	49	334	391	344
Usage						
Exports	330	386	215	10	10	7
Final use	1,076	1,076	800	520	520	377
Inputs	76	74	51	444	407	280

On this basis the manufacturing position looks distinctly more plausible, though it still postulates a considerable amount of import substitution. The need for a radical increase in agricultural production is all the more urgent, implying an annual increase of 4 per cent a year: the greater part of the increase is still needed to meet the increase in final use (i.e. fundamentally food), but the additional exports are crucial to the success of the economy.

Notes on statistics

1. Distribution and transport of goods is regarded as a service, bought separately by the purchaser, except in the case of exports (see 3 below).

2. All internal transactions are recorded at 'producers prices', including taxes, in millions of old Cedis (see 3 below for imports).

3. In order to link with the international payments statistics, *imports* are given c.i.f. and the import tax on them is regarded as value added in the first process of manufacture or distribution which follows. *Exports* are f.o.b., and the costs of transport and distribution are regarded as bought by the producer.

4. The figures for 1965 used in Table 21 of the World Bank Report dated March 1967 (pages 102 to 104) are regarded as authoritative. In particular, the figure for imports of goods (404 million old Cedis c.i.f.) exceeds the sum of the details given in the trade returns by 20 million Cedis, and this difference is assumed to consist of manufactures (possibly ships and aircraft).

5. In making break-downs for 1965 much use was made of figures in the Economic Survey, 1965 (with later additions supplied by the Central Bureau of Statistics) and of 'Ghana's Economy and aid requirements in 1967'. Imagination was freely used to fill in gaps and to convert from one basic to another.

6. The 1975 figures are based on the World Bank projections for 1975 and the analysis developed for 1965: the *relationships* between figures for the two years are more reliable than the absolute figures.

7. The change of exchange rate is simply ignored, since the exercise is essentially one at constant 1965 prices. In order to see the foreign exchange effect of the 1975 prices for international transactions, the old exchange rate should be used.

Note

This paper was written in July 1967 at the end of a period of three-months which the author spent in Ghana as a member of the Harvard Development Advisory Service. It has not been amended to take account of developments that have occurred since that time.

Notes

1 Strictly speaking, this calculation requires the insertion of minor figures for Ghana's exports and imports of services. The starting figure is converted from Cedis at the old rate of exchange, as it reflects transactions done at world prices.

  It is an implicit assumption of the Bank's 'financial' approach that there will be sufficient adaptability in the Ghanaian structure of production to ensure that this amount of imports will enable the economy to produce on the assumed scale, rather than suffer from shortages of key materials etc. (This is the subject which we are trying to investigate.)

2 Rather unsatisfactorily, devaluation is simply ignored: the figures are taken to represent quantities of goods at constant prices.

3 The actual procedure involved a very slight amount of iteration. Knowing that the gross domestic product had risen by 44 per cent and assuming that manufacture would have doubled, a provisional figure for the total of the input items was entered. This agreed to within one unit with the sum of the final figures, so for purposes of exposition we assume that the first figure was exact. In splitting the total for mining between home production and imports, it was assumed that the input of crude oil would still be wholly imported.

J. B. K. HUNTER

The Development of the Labour Market in Kenya

I

The development of the labour market began, effectively, in the 1890s, with the building of the railroad from the Coast to Lake Victoria, largely by imported Indian workers. From then on, urban development was polarized almost entirely at the ocean terminal, Mombasa, and at Nairobi, which became the headquarters of the railway administration and the territorial government. Both these were staffed by British officials and British and Indian skilled and semi-skilled personnel; for many of the unskilled jobs Africans were recruited. British and Indian immigrants developed the social overhead capital and early manufacturing and commerce of the colony, and with the influx of European 'settlers' from the early years of the twentieth century as planters and farmers, forming 'enclaves' in the customary tribal land and subsistence pattern of the Africans, there were established very early on the features of the developing labour market which remained almost universal till the second world war and characteristic till the last few years. Ownership of modern capital, enterprise in the money economy and management of its growth sectors were the function of immigrants; commerce and small-scale services, except for local enterprise among Africans in the 'reserves', was largely the function of the Asians – immigrants and, later, also those born in Kenya; clerical and artisan skills were also a preserve of Europeans and Asians. Africans provided the great bulk of the unskilled labour. Development of the labour market was more complex than simple models of economic dualism might imply, but is most easily and usefully described in their terms.

Commercial farming, in the hands of a relatively small number of Europeans at its prewar peak, was the source of most employment for Africans. Its production was for export or for the increasing, relatively high-income local European and Asian communities, not for the Africans, whose purchasing power was not, therefore, an important factor for employers in this respect. For most farmers, especially in the early pioneering years, it was a 'hard slog' and a risky venture. Most had relatively little experience; in most cases their efficiency of use of land and capacity to adapt and innovate, was probably not high; their efficiency of use of labour, from both technical and economic viewpoints, was conditioned by the apparent availability, at least potentially and most of the time in fact, of 'unlimited' supplies of African labour for outdoor and indoor service from surrounding smallholdings or recruited from further afield. The labour was inexperienced, relatively little became 'permanent' – though this varied greatly – usually 'migratory', temporary, seasonal or casual. Large reliance on daily and ticket contracts reflected this, as did the provisions of the Masters and Servants Ordinances of 1906 and 1910. Turnover was very high, possibilities of 'on the job training' small and hence, for the most part, unconsidered; in many cases there was probably also simple incomprehension of the possibility of Africans learning skills, and feeling that if they did they would cause friction. The concept of the short-term 'target' African labourer (and the 'backward sloping supply curve', so to speak), which was probably realistic for a time, became almost universal, as did that of the 'lazy African'. These attitudes persisted widely in agriculture particularly until the 1950s. But wages were low in absolute terms, even though they did vary according to demand and supply conditions. When pressure of demand tended to ease up wage rates, settlers tried to get the taxes on Africans raised and asked for pressure from DOs to stimulate supply (with indifferent success, on the whole). Later, as population put pressure on land in the main African tribal areas, and the question of land-ownership became the main focus of interracial tension and political development among Africans, the system of 'squatters' added to the supply of labour just when the impact of instability and depression in export markets was restricting activity in the commercial farming sector, and therefore demand for labour. New crops were developed over time, and new methods, but in general throughout the interwar period, technical production functions remained fairly static. Expansion and contraction of production was achieved by more or less proportionate movements in the size of the labour force; productivity remained low; African labour was almost universally undifferentiated and unskilled. In other sectors of the developing labour market, both private – and public – this was also largely true. One result was perhaps that with most Africans the concept of paid employment as a 'career' – as anything but a means of earning cash for fairly short-term needs – was relatively slow in developing.

The second world war brought a relative shortage of labour in all sectors. This was partly caused by recruitment of Africans to the forces, where many acquired some education and skills as drivers, mechanics and clerks. It was also due to the relative prosperity of subsistence-cum-cash-sales smallholding agriculture as prices rose. Political consciousness among African communities increased. While most Europeans probably looked on these effects as temporary phenomena, in the event the war proved to have radically speeded up trends which had been just beginning to develop on a very small scale in the main urban centres before it.

II

After the war and in the 1950s there was comparatively rapid growth and development in Kenya. This was stimulated by favourable export prices and by further immigration of Europeans and Asians which greatly increased the home market for the products of the 'modern' sectors. Cash incomes of Africans too were becoming a significant factor for these sectors. Paradoxically, perhaps, the Emergency of 1952–55, while it disrupted the labour market to some extent, brought further inflows of capital and people with high purchasing power.

The major effects on the labour market are indicated by tables 1 and 2. Total paid employment, as shown by the Annual Enumeration of Employment, expanded by 48 per cent between 1948 and its peak in 1960. At the time it was thought that numbers employed were a rising proportion of total population, but the 1962 Census of Population showed that population had risen faster than had been estimated. Enumerated employees remained about 7·7 per cent of the total.

Employment in commercial, relatively large-scale *agriculture*, rose by some 40 per cent, but steadily throughout the period. Within this sector the relatively small numbers of Europeans and Asians – the managerial and skilled elements – rose very much faster. This sector provided 46 per cent of jobs in 1948 and 43 per cent in 1960. In *private industry and commerce*, enumerated employment expanded by 52 per cent – again with the European and Asian rates of growth much faster. This sector accounted for fractionally under 30 per cent of jobs in 1948 and fractionally over 30 per cent in 1960. Employment in the *public sector* rose from 24 per cent of the total in 1948 to 26 per cent in 1960 – an expansion of 58 per cent in numbers employed. Here, the European element almost doubled but, significantly, Asian employment rose only 37 per cent. Employment in both the private non-agriculture sector and the public services reached a peak in 1957 and then declined slightly – the main declines being in African employment.

In commercial agriculture diversification of products and methods increased, but on the whole it was still the case that expansion was achieved largely by expansion of the labour force, especially the

118

TABLE 1 Reported employment and earnings 1948–65[4]

	Numbers employed[1] ('000s)					Estimated annual wage bill[2] (£m)				
	1948	1957	1960	1963	1965	1948	1957	1960	1963	1965
Agriculture & forestry										
African	192·6	251·1	269·1	217·6	207·6	3·3	8·4	10·0	10·1	10·5
Asian	0·3	0·5	0·8	0·7	0·7	0·1	0·2	0·4	0·4	0·5
European	1·0	1·8	1·9	1·4	1·1	0·6	2·0	2·1	1·6	1·7
Total	193·9	253·7	271·8	219·7	209·5	4·0	10·6	12·5	12·1	12·7
Private industry & commerce (including domestic service)										
African	103·9	156·8	151·1	121·8	169·3	3·3	12·6	13·9	16·1	23·4
Asian	14·6	25·8	25·6	24·3	27·4	3·7	11·5	11·7	12·5	15·7
European	6·0	11·4	12·3	10·2	9·5	3·6	12·6	14·5	14·5	15·3
Total	124·5	194·0	189·0	156·3	206·2	10·6	36·7	40·1	43·1	54·4
Public services[3]										
African	89·0	146·9	140·7	139·5	165·8	3·2	12·5	14·4	19·2	32·8
Asian	8·6	10·9	11·8	11·7	7·8	2·3	6·1	6·6	7·7	6·4
European	4·5	9·2	8·9	6·1	4·5	2·8	11·0	11·3	9·6	7·5
Total	102·1	167·0	161·4	157·3	178·1	8·3	29·6	32·3	36·5	46·6
All										
African	385·5	554·8	560·9	478·9	542·8	9·8	33·5	38·3	45·4	66·7
Asian	23·5	37·2	38·3	36·7	35·9	6·1	17·8	18·7	20·6	22·5
European	11·5	22·4	23·0	17·7	15·0	7·0	25·6	27·9	25·7	24·5
Total	420·5	614·4	622·2	533·3	593·7	22·9	76·9	84·9	91·7	113·7

[1] Includes casual, part-time and apprentices as reported in the Annual Enumerations. Employment does not include self-employed.
[2] Wage bill: all cash payments including estimates of employers' contribution to housing, value of rations and free board.
[3] Public services: include Central Government, local authorities. EACSO employees in Kenya, locally recruited staffs of foreign governments; EAR&H, (Kenya); EAP&T (Kenya).
[4] Figures not always strictly comparable over time, but this does not affect the general pattern. After 1963 coverage was extended in rural areas; this resulted in an addition of about 42,000 employees in the private industry and commerce sector. The Economic Survey 1967 (table 7.1) gives slightly amended figures of employment for 1965: 28,300, almost entirely Africans. It also adds an estimate of 'unreported employment' for 1965: 28,300, almost entirely Africans.
Source: *Reported Employment and Wages in Kenya 1948–60* tables 2, 12. *Statistical Abstract 1966* tables 147(a), 147(b).

TABLE 2   Average annual earnings 1948–65 (£)

	1948	1957	1960	1963	1965
Agriculture & forestry					
African	17	33	37	46	50
Asian	333	400	500	571	714
European	600	1,111	1,100	1,143	1,546
Private industry & commerce (including domestic service)					
African	32	80	92	132	138
Asian	254	445	457	515	573
European	600	1,105	1,180	1,421	1,610
Public service					
African	36	85	102	137	197
Asian	267	560	559	658	820
European	622	1,195	1,270	1,574	1,666
All					
African	25	60	68	95	123
Asian	260	478	488	561	627
European	609	1,145	1,233	1,452	1,633

Wages and salaries are usually quoted in terms of shillings per month in
East Africa £20 p.a.= 33s. per month
£36 p.a.= 60s. per month
£60 p.a.=100s. per month

Source: calculated from table 1

TABLE 3   Population growth ('000s)

	1948 census	1962 census	1965 (est.)
Africa	5,251	8,366	9,097
Asian	125	215	226
European	30	55	42
Total	5,406	8,636	9,365

Source: Statistical Abstract 1966 tables 10 and 11.

unskilled labour force; especially in labour-intensive crop sectors like coffee, sisal and to a lesser extent tea. Attempts to stabilize the labour force went further on some plantations and mixed farms, and African headmen became even more important than before; 'permanent cores' of workers were given land and housing (of very variable quality), and their families provided both domestic service and seasonal supplementation of the labour force, so that use of 'outside' labour seasonally could be restricted. With the spread of elementary education among Africans some Africans were recruited as clerical workers, while others obtained some degree of technical skills by on-the-job-learning. But such cases were still exceptional. In most cases effective supervision was done by Europeans and artisan and clerical jobs by either Europeans or Asians. The bulk of the African labour was still, in terms of skill, effectively 'undifferentiated', and turnover of labour remained relatively high. In the late 1950s, indeed, it may have risen as the Swynnerton Plan for consolidation and expansion of smallholder agriculture, with opportunities for cash earnings as well as subsistence, developed. In commercial agriculture average earnings remained low and rose relatively slowly, though the provision of land particularly increased real earnings. Labour was still regarded as relatively 'cheap', and only rather slowly was its relatively high 'effective cost' beginning to affect methods.

In general, employment for Africans in the developing and diversifying private industrial and commercial sector (which included domestic service) was also unskilled, and artisan and clerical skills were the function of Asians and Europeans in it too. But for Africans, much more differentiation and opportunity to acquire skills and use them developed in the 1950s. The stimulus to this was the advent and expansion of relatively large, 'modern' manufacturing firms, using technologically advanced methods. For them, at least in 'central manufacturing' processes, low-wage unskilled labour was *not* cheap. The problems of turnover and supervision were serious from the start, while experience of training and employing Africans with some skills of the technically more advanced kind were involved, was relatively encouraging. Attempts to reduce turnover and increase skills by recruiting Africans with some education and vocational training and by offering relatively attractive wages became a cautious but growing policy, and competition among firms for scarce skilled and 'committed' labour was important as a stimulus. Most firms relied on some form of 'on the job' training; a few larger ones developed small training schools for their own employees; use of the government trade testing centre began to spread.

In the public sector this was also true. East African Railways & Harbours, through its training school, had been training Africans for many years. In 1955 the Civil Service in general was thrown open to people of all races, and by the end of the 1950s a relatively small but significant number of Africans were climbing the ladders of the administrative civil service in both urban and rural areas, and numbers were expanding in clerical grades as well as in local government and primary school-teaching in the state sector (Africans had been teaching in private tribal schools before the War.) By the late 1950s Africans were competing effectively with Asians for posts in the public sector – as the relative rise in average earnings would suggest.

Average African earnings in employment as a whole rose by about 170 per cent from 1948 to 1960. How much of a rise in real terms this meant is uncertain. The only cost of living index, for Nairobi, rose 60 per cent, but was certainly not a guide to African cost of living changes. On the whole it is likely that costs of living for Africans rose less than this. In the mid-1950s it was probably still the case that average *real* incomes of agricultural employees were not very much less than those of wage-earners in other sectors, in Nairobi and Mombasa where development and employment tended to be concentrated, and in smaller urban centres. But the 'gap' was widening. In general it remained true that perhaps the bulk of African workers in urban centres were essentially short-term migrants, and therefore, for the most part, likely to remain unskilled.

The Ministry of Labour developed employment exchanges, and government intervention in the labour market took three main forms: first, the rising employment of Africans; second, the spread of state schooling – primary and to a small extent secondary – for African communities (previously this had been provided, if at all, by the churches and by Africans themselves), and attempts to encourage the spread of technical skills, particularly among Africans, by the development of a Government Trade Testing Centre in Nairobi in the early 1950s, the expansion of technical schools and eventually the establishment of the Kenya Polytechnic in Nairobi in 1960. In terms of numbers trained vocationally the effects were small, but they were significant. Third, the development of minimum wages. These stemmed originally from wartime labour problems in Nairobi and Mombasa. In 1944 statutory minimum wages were introduced in Nairobi. In 1946 a Minimum Wages Ordinance was applied to Nairobi and Mombasa, and minimum wages were soon extended to seven other small urban centres. In 1951 a reconstituted Minimum Wages Advisory Board included workers' representatives for the first time. The urban minimum wages were based on the assumed needs of single men in the urban centres without family responsibilities; on the assumption of unskilled, migratory labour. In 1946 a South African expert, in comments on an investigation into industrial unrest in Mombasa, had envisaged the need for eventual statutory minima based on 'family' needs. In 1954 the very influential Carpenter Committee Report was published. Its general philosophy of moving towards a 'high wage economy' even at the possible cost of restricting the growth of the labour force – the first real avowal of this outlook in Kenya – became important almost at once. It recommended a broadening of the basis of calculation of the single man's minimum wage, including both 'povery datum line' and 'human needs' factors; it also recommended the conversion of the minimum wage to a family basis, assessed at 250 per cent of the single-man basis, by annual increments over ten years, with the aim of furthering the development of a permanent, stabilised labour force divorced from the 'reserves'. The government accepted the principle, but, for financial reasons, not the target; but it did accept the idea of a statutory minimum wage, based on the needs of a man and wife only, at 67 per cent above the 'youth' minimum, and proposed to move to this target over five years. As minimum wages were revised the adult rate was adjusted upwards, but by 1960 the adjustment factor was still only 1.3. (In 1962 the Carpenter basis of calculation was abandoned and an expenditure survey basis was substituted, but the 'Carpenter objective' is still influential in Kenya.) The Committee's further recommendation – a rural minimum wage – was not accepted for the time being in the mid-1950s. Fourth, as in other British colonies, the government accepted that voluntary collective bargaining between trade unions and employers (individually or in associations) on the British model, with provision for conciliation and arbitration by the Ministry of Labour where necessary, was a desirable objective, provided that trade unions were registered, were viable, and were not used for political agitation. Characteristically the Ministry of Labour's objective was to encourage organic growth of unions from the grass-roots upwards, through the development of joint consultation in works councils to begin with, as a way of getting experience and defining and restricting objectives and methods. In the meantime, and (as in Britain) in principle as a temporary measure, wages councils were established in several industries.

Some trade unions had already emerged in the 1940s. In 1950 the Kenya Federation of Registered Trade Unions (with five unions affiliated) was formed. In 1953 T.J.Mboya of the Local Government Workers' Union became its general secretary, a position he held when it was renamed the Kenya Federation of Labour in 1955. His energetic leadership and considerable organising and negotiating ability, combined with carefulness in stressing the 'professional' objectives of the unions even while in effect they were to a large extent taking the political place of the proscribed political parties, was one of the major factors – possibly the dominant factor given the great scarcity of experience and organisational ability that the trade unions faced at the time – in determining and shaping the growth of unions and union policies in the next few years. The British Colonial Office and Ministry of Labour, the TUC, the American AFL/CIO, the ILO and the ICFTU, to which KFL affiliated, were all influential, as were several foreign advisers. One major departure from the British model, on the advice of the ICFTU, was the adoption of 'industrial unionism', which the Registrar of Trade Unions accepted – several previous unions had shown tendencies to try to develop as 'general unions'. This certainly did not remove all problems of jurisdiction and causes of inter-union friction, but it simplified later development considerably. In 1956 an Association of Commercial & Industrial Employers was formed in Nairobi; in 1957 it became the Kenya-wide Federation of Kenya Employers. This body encouraged the development of employers' associations in different industries and the acceptance of the need to recognise and negotiate with 'responsible' and viable trade unions; it also undertook to advise and to represent its affiliates in negotiations where this was wanted. In November 1957 an agreement between KFL and FKE laid down the basis of development for the future.

III

Kenya became independent in December 1963. The years just before and after that were years of difficult political, economic and social adjustment, which had its counterpart in the labour market. GDP in monetary terms stagnated in 1960 to 1962, apart from a slight rise in output in the public sector and a sharp rise in the value of output outside the recorded monetary economy. Since 1963, however, private industry and commerce and the public sector have expanded output quite rapidly, while total agricultural production, in money terms, hardly changed until there came a sharp rise in 1966. The moderate rate of growth in the 1960s has masked a good deal of development in all sectors, but notably in manufacturing, commerce and services. Located mainly in and around Nairobi, development has produced a rapidly widening range of products, of technology, of skills required and job opportunities, prospects of promotion and relatively very high salaries for young Africans. The period has been one of rapidly rising wages and – till 1965 – considerable industrial unrest.

Tables 1 and 2 give very generally the trends in employment and average earnings. They help to indicate major features of the labour market in the 1960s.

The failure of total paid employment to grow

This is a problem now characteristic of many developing countries. In Kenya, total population has been rising at some 3 per cent per annum, but total recorded employment (which excludes self-employment) fell from the peak of 1960 until 1965, when it covered 6·5 per cent of population – even though, from 1964 on, extended coverage by the annual Enumeration of Employment has added many more employees in small-scale rural non-agricultural enterprises (42,000 in 1964). Estimates of unrecorded employment (almost all in small-scale African services) raised the 1965 total to 619,000. Apart from this there are appreciable numbers of wage earners in smallholding agriculture for which accurate figures are not available. For 1966 the Economic Survey (table 7.1) gives recorded employment as 603,100, estimated unrecorded as 31,600 (total 634,700), and estimates that there were over 100,000 wage employees (for the most part, perhaps, employed on a casual or seasonal basis) in very small-scale agriculture in and outside settlement schemes, and in fishing. It seems possible that there is also quite substantial under-reporting of employment in towns, which are growing faster than their recorded employment totals; part of the 'gap' is no doubt families, but this is unlikely to explain it all. At any rate total employment now seems to be expanding once more.

The reasons for the failure of employment to expand have been a matter for concern and discussion in Kenya since the late 1950s. They led, for one thing, to an attempt to investigate unemployment in 1960. To some extent the trend has been misleading for the decline has been partly offset by a rise in self-employment in smallholder agriculture in the settlement schemes and elsewhere, and probably also in other small scale activites. But the reasons for the decline appear to have been mainly associated with political developments.

(a) In the early and mid-1950s expansion of capacity in manufacturing, commerce and services went ahead of demand, producing a bunching effect, and the later 1950s were a period of growing capacity-use in which the need for labour did not rise proportionately; then at the end of the 1950s there was another, relatively smaller, spurt of expansion of capacity, involving temporary expansion of building and construction; building and construction which had been partly stimulated by the Emergency earlier, had contracted fairly sharply in the later 1950s. In the early 1960s building and construction stagnated during years of political uncertainty – employment in the industry fell from 21,000 in 1960 to 8,600 in 1963. Only recently has demand for housing and other large scale construction begun to rise sharply again, and this is leading now to a serious shortage especially of skilled artisans. Similarly employment in manufacturing and repairs fell sharply from 52,300 in 1960 to 40,700 in 1965, then began to rise.

(b) Since 1960 the main reason for the contraction of total employment has been its contraction in large-scale agriculture – plantations and mixed farms. This has been largely caused by the departure of many European farmers and estate owners, the inevitable delay in replacing them by large African farmers or smallholder agriculture, and the fact that while African farming, both large- and small-scale, tends to be more labour-intensive both in crops and in methods, initial difficulties of development, managerial inexperience and debt-burdens mean a contraction of total paid employment, which is offset to some extent by numbers of self-employed and by use of much more flexible family labour. Apart from this, world prices for export crops have on the whole been unfavourable, while costs of production have tended to rise. Sisal in particular has contracted in Kenya for this reason, but coffee has also been affected. On the other hand, smallholder African production of coffee, sisal, tea, etc., has risen; here too there has probably been a shift of wage employment from larger to smaller farms, but also contraction.

(c) It seems clear that since the 1950s, while the number of firms engaged in private industry, and commerce has increased, there has been a growing tendency to economise especially on the employment of unskilled labour, by increasing mechanisation in manufacturing and, to a lesser extent, ancillary processes, and by organisational changes. The newer methods tend to be more skill-intensive. The Emergency itself, during which Kikuyu workers in Nairobi – the vast majority of employees in the city at the time – were removed, probably had a 'shock effect' on employers' attitudes to use of labour, even though workers from other tribes came to the city to replace the Kikuyu. Later, in the 1950s and early 1960s as the objective of a 'high wage economy', which KFL, FKE, and the Ministry of Labour all supported, became more operative, wage increases, especially for labourers, and shorter hours, higher housing and other allowances and the relatively high cost of supervision of un-skilled and lowly-skilled workers, or workers with higher formal qualifications but little experience, all raised effective costs and brought continuing re-examination of productivity and technical and organisational methods, and this attitude has widened and remained. It has been most important, perhaps, in larger-scale, modern-technology firms. These in any case, either as subsidiaries of foreign groups or through knowledge of methods employed in more developed economies, do seem to have an inbuilt tendency to adapt advanced technology, especially when beginning new ventures. (But adoption of advanced technology still tends to be accompanied by considerably greater use of labour than would be used with the same technology in a more developed country.) The effective costs of low-skilled or inexperienced labour have been an added incentive, even where it would be possible to raise prices to the home market. So too, perhaps, was the period of considerable industrial unrest associated with confused developments in trade unions in the immediate post-Independence period. In cases of many incoming firms this economy in the use of labour per unit of output has been offset, in terms of total employment, by rapid initial growth. In the case of some old-established enterprises in both private and public sectors it has meant a contraction in total employment, at least during the period of relative stagnation. In the publicly-owned Mombasa Docks the tendency has been less evident, in spite of very high and rapidly increasing wages in the early 60s. In large-scale European agriculture since 1960, rising effective costs of labour, given the effective 'ceiling' imposed by export prices, have also brought trends towards economising on labour. Most notable was the effect of the Industrial Court's 'Coffee Award' early in 1966, when a rise of 25 per cent in wage rates was followed by large-scale redundancy. The effects of wage and other increases in small-scale manufacturing, shops, repairs, transport, etc., are much more difficult to assess because of almost complete lack of information, but more use of 'family' labour and casual labour may have been one fairly common response.

(*d*) Apart from political changes and minimum wages, government policy in itself has probably had little effect. The tax system incorporates capital allowances, not geared to employment. This may have had some effect, though it is unlikely to have been a major one.

Growing complexity and disparities in the labour market

Between 1960 and 1965, in the paid-employment part of the economy, average earnings of Africans rose by over 80 per cent, at a cumulative annual rate of about 13 per cent. These increases were due mainly to increases in the statutory minimum wage rates and rates for labourers determined by wages councils and by normal collective bargaining; also to increases in higher wages and salaries, and to the extensive movement of Africans into higher paid jobs than before, particularly in the public sector, and to movements up incremental scales in that sector and in the firms in the private sector which also operate incremental scales. The racial disparities – a legacy from the past, but still grounded largely in differences in skills and occupations – remained, but were reduced, except in agriculture. The reduction was largest in the public sector, which was largely Africanised during the period. In the private sector increases in earnings were fastest before Independence and then slowed (though this is not true of all firms). In public service the increase in the early 1960s was slower than in private industry and commerce, but from 1963 to 1965 very much faster. Since 1965 wages in reported employment have been rising at about 7 per cent per annum.

These increases certainly represent an appreciable rise in average *real* earnings. Between 1960 and 1965 the Nairobi Wage Earners' Index rose by about 11·5 per cent. Though the adequacy of the basis of this index may be open to increasing doubt and it is not representative of wage-earners in other urban areas or in rural areas, it probably gives a reasonable indication of the general pattern of the cost of living. The Salaries Review Commission of 1967 noted (Report, p. 16) that average real earnings of Africans rose by 75 per cent between 1958 and 1965; by almost 100 per cent in the public sector.

In a developing country one might expect to find wide differentials due to 'market imperfections' as well as to social and racial structure and to personal abilities: differentials for education and skills, differentials between agriculture and industry and commerce, differentials within sectors according to size and 'modernity' of enterprises and degree of trade union activity, perhaps differentials between public and private sectors, and, most probably, a growing gap between urban and rural sectors, and especially between urban wage and salary earners and subsistence farmers. The development process may be expected to widen many of these differentials in the early stages, the more rapidly it takes place, and later, with general social and economic development, they may be expected to narrow again. In general the Kenya labour market in the last few years appears to illustrate these hypotheses.

Differentials based on education and skills. In Nairobi the statutory minimum wage for adults rose from 95s. + 24s./50c. housing allowance at the beginning of 1960 to 115s. + 35s. in 1963 – a rise of 21 per cent in the wage and 25 per cent in the gross total. Rates in other urban areas and for youths differed in levels, but increases were of the same order. The minimum wage was then held, despite increasing demands for revision, until July 1967, when it was raised in Nairobi to 175s. gross (with reductions if housing is provided, and elimination of the 'youth' differential). Rates for unskilled labourers established by

Wages Councils have varied between industries but have, of course, been appreciably above the statutory area minimum rates; between 1963 and 1967 they were increased by over 20 per cent on average. Labourers' rates established in the public sector have also been significantly above the statutory minimum. In private industry and commerce the rates for unskilled labourers in small enterprises – according to very fragmentary evidence – have varied considerably, but appear to have been either wages council minima or above; while rates in larger firms are all appreciably above the statutory minimum – ranging from the Mombasa Docks, where in 1965–6 the starting rate for completely unskilled labourers was about twice the gross statutory Mombasa minimum rate (and higher than many workers with some degree of skill were receiving there or in Nairobi), and starting rates not very much lower in one or two other firms, to rates of 190s. or 200s. (plus housing allowance), which seemed to be accepted by new, small but 'modern' firms in 1966 as the lowest rate they could reasonably pay. However, the category 'general labourer' is itself rather a wide one, too undifferentiated. Implicit in labourers' rates established by collective bargaining is that firms will select recruits according to personal attributes, experience of industrial conditions, competence and so on, will 'pay more' for such men, and, if necessary will become more selective in recruitment.

These increases have tended, on the whole to compress differentials at the foot of the wages and salary scales in all sectors. Above them, differentials for 'skills' are wide, especially for 'middle-level' skills in clerical, secretarial and artisan grades. They are much wider than one would expect in more developed countries, reflecting, of course, the supply and demand relationship particularly as it applies to Africans. Entrance qualifications for skilled grades tend to be based, in both private and public sectors, on educational levels in the first place. Thus a small firm or farm recruiting a clerk might offer a considerable differential to recruits who had passed KPE – the Kenya Preliminary Examination for entrance to secondary education (many who pass cannot find places in schools) – and considerably more, if it could afford it, for recruits with some secondary schooling. Larger firms would demand a higher initial level of education but offer similarly wide differentials. For artisan and secretarial grades, both wages councils and collective bargaining tie rates to vocational training qualifications. The Government Trade Tests have come to be accepted widely for artisan grades in this respect, and the differentials involved are wide; (and in larger firms and the public sector, with higher wage rates go higher allowances, in general).

On the whole, even though there is a relative shortage of 'middle-level' clerical and artisan skills, and rising demand for them suggests that for the time being this shortage is even increasing, the negotiated *rates* do not seem to have widened differentials in the last few years. Indeed in both wages councils and collective bargaining the tendency has been rather to negotiate flat percentage increases for all grades of labour, or actually smaller increases in rates for higher paid workers. The industrial unions were in most cases very largely concerned with the wages of the lower-paid who usually formed the bulk of their membership, and wages council members too have been primarily concerned with the needs of the poorest workers, although in one or two cases shortages of particular grades of labour apparently caused wages councils to widen the differential in their favour.

In practice, however, both private firms and government departments, in search of greater competence and lower costs of turnover and supervision, appear to have been informally upgrading the educational and vocational qualifications for entry and promotion to levels above the established formal minima, and have been offering opportunities of more rapid internal upgrading to competent, experienced workers. This is partly because some of the 'paper qualifications' obtained, particularly perhaps by girls who train in some of the numerous private secretarial colleges which have developed in the last few years, are themselves very inadequate indications of competence. A really competent woman secretary in a large private firm can therefore earn very much more than in say the UK in a similar position, while even quite small firms who can will offer unexpectedly high wages to book-keepers and secretaries, who, in many cases, play a much more important rôle in the firm than they would in a country where their skills are more common. In addition, incremental scales are used by some firms, though the general policy of the FKE is to establish the 'rate for the job' and a 'clean wage' rather than the traditional patterns of wages, increments, allowances of various kinds. In practice, therefore, the relative established rates do not necessarily reflect the actual differentials.

Private industry and commerce. The pattern of differentials as between industries and firms is very complex and only partially known. Wages (and accompanying allowances of various kinds which are commonly negotiated in comprehensive agreements by collective bargaining, as they are in wages councils) for similar occupations and grades of skill have varied very widely among industries, and, within industries, among firms of different sizes and different technical and organisational methods. Small firms obtaining help from the ICDC, according to investigations by Peter Marris, appeared to pay rates at or above the statutory or wages council minima –

K

sometimes considerably above. About the very large number of small Asian and African shops, repair shops and other small enterprises, very little is known. There have been few complaints to the Ministry of Labour about firms paying less than the minima, but this in itself may not be conclusive evidence, and the prevalence of the family firm with its flexible capacity in labour supply and use of casual labour in situations where there is no shortage of men and boys looking for casual jobs, make it very difficult to find and evaluate evidence. Most larger firms in all industries have become members of employers' associations or directly of the FKE. The FKE has been encouraging the use of job classification and job evaluation as a means of simplifying and rationalising wage structures, by negotiation with unions, and *within* some industries, at least among larger firms, there is considerable uniformity, but not, unfortunately, between different industries. But the uniformity of job classification has not meant uniformity of rates paid, and the trade unions' general policy of concentrating on larger firms and basing wage claims essentially on their presumed 'ability to pay' has tended to maintain disparities, even though, having obtained wage increases from one firm in an industry, unions have then sometimes used the argument of comparability as between firms in claiming from another. Larger companies, and smaller 'modern' firms, especially if foreign owned, have been both rather better able to pay higher rates, by economising on labour if necessary, and also, on the whole, more prepared to accept the arguments for doing so – both the stabilisation of the work force argument and the argument that wages, especially of the lower-paid, are still too low to meet reasonable family needs.

Commercial Agriculture. Not till 1965 was a general minimum wage fixed for agriculture by Wages Regulation (at 60s. per month on monthly contracts, with proportionate rates for 'ticket' and daily terms; *less* defined deductions for food or land given; housing has to be provided free). But in 1961 a minimum wage was established in general agriculture by collective bargaining between the Kenya National Farmers' Union and the (then) General and Agricultural Workers Union; the rate then agreed has been raised since. In plantation agriculture – coffee, sisal, tea, sugar – collective bargaining also established minimum rates which have risen since. There is rather less complexity in agriculture than in industry and commerce, at least among larger firms, but the same sort of pattern as in the non-agricultural private sector applies. Rates of wages and allowances have been much lower on average than in industry and commerce, and, compared with most larger manufacturing and commercial firms, there has probably been a stricter 'ceiling' on costs, imposed by world prices. In general, actual wages appear to have approximated more closely to the established basic rates. Most larger plantations and farms became members of employers' associations and FKE, and accepted the need to negotiate fairly comprehensive agreements with the appropriate union. Probably a majority have been paying more than minimum rates and the others either the rates or just below, though lower cash payments may be offset by the provision of more land and/or food. Some of the African newcomers to large-scale farming in these initial years have had land to spare and have made it available to employees, and the value of land, given its growing scarcity, may in fact be considerably higher than the deductions allowable by wages regulations or collective agreements.

In general, increases in agricultural rates have been relatively small, especially in recent years. The 'coffee award' of early 1966 was exceptional. The moderate rises have been largely because of the difficulties posed by unfavourable prices in export markets – there has been no increase in the sisal industry for several years now, and the Union has accepted the need for this. But, as in commerce and manufacturing industry, there have been quite wide variations between agricultural industries themselves in rates for comparable jobs.

Small farms present just as difficult a problem of evaluation as do small firms outside agriculture. They have tended to have relatively heavy debt burdens in their initial years, and these make cash wages a disproportionately high cost, so that a fairly general response may have been to rely heavily on family labour and the possibilities of getting casual labour which are inherent in subsistence farming. There may have been widespread less-than-legal-minimum cash payment, and the KPAWU has had neither the organisation nor the resources, nor perhaps the interest at local level, to play the inspecting and representative role even with regard to larger farms, which some unions have been more able to attempt in the urban centres and with certain industries established in rural areas.

The public sector. Wage and salary rates are the subject of collective bargaining and periodic commissions of inquiry. There has been greater uniformity of rates and also, perhaps, of actual earnings on a 'job for job' basis in the public services but, in these too, differentials have been rather wide and varying, e.g. between central and local governments, and among local authorities. The public sector is 'dominant' in the labour market in the sense that it is responsible for some 30 per cent of all paid employment and some 50 per cent of jobs outside agriculture. But the relationship of wages and salaries between it and the private sector has not been clear. This has been partly because of difficulties of comparing occupations, partly because public salaries have been revised less regularly; also because of the less widespread use of incremental scales in the private sector, and because of the 'status' that has attached to employment in the civil service.

In both sectors the traditional influence of 'expatriate' salaries for senior officials, managers, professional men and very skilled technicians has no doubt helped to widen differentials,but even without this 'market' tendencies would almost certainly have produced very wide differences in any case. Though little is known about the pay of highly-paid Africans in large private companies, it seems clear that in many cases their rates and prospects (even if reduced from 'expatriate' levels, as may happen) are very much higher than those of senior civil servants. In general, large, 'modern' private firms can and do pay more in cash and fringe benefits on a 'job for job' comparison than does the civil service, for senior executives, middle-grade and even low-paid ranks. But this is not true of the bulk of smaller firms.

It may be that the rapid rise of earnings and prospects of upgrading and promotion in the public service are slowing down, even though there are still shortages at senior administrative and middle-grade levels. Ceilings on public recurrent expenditure have certainly hit many local authorities. There has been much redundancy among primary schoolteachers in several of the rural areas, and refusal to grant increases to teachers – the 'least skilled' of whom are very poorly paid – has been one of the main issues of industrial dispute in the last few years. Other local authority employees who have been awarded increases by commission or arbitration have not received them because the central government has declined to provide the extra grants; this caused strikes in Nairobi and elsewhere in 1967. The government's recent decision to require Nairobi and Mombasa to hand over 50 per cent of their Graduated Personal Tax proceeds (a tax levied by local authorities for their local purposes throughout the country) to the Treasury, with the object of channelling more funds to poorer communities, is likely to harden the 'ceiling' against income increases or to involve tedundancy. In 1967 the Salaries Review Commission recommended a virtual standstill on salaries except for schoolteachers and very low-paid employees (though its recommendation of increased housing allowances during the present period of shortage of houses and very high rents, especially in Nairobi, seemed to offset its general insistence on 'restraint'). If Africanisation of the higher grades of the private sector goes rapidly ahead, there may well be considerable turnover in senior and middle grades in the public sector; this has already been a problem for several departments.

The 'Urban-Rural Gap'. Differences in cash incomes and in most conditions of service between broadly urban (especially Nairobi and Mombasa) and rural employment have widened since the middle 1950s, and seem likely to continue to widen. They have been only partly offset by the provision of land to agricultural employees, even though the real value of such land has probably been rising significantly; in any case many urban employees of all ranks retain shambas in rural areas, farmed by relatives, and the desire to retain such contact with the land seems to have been little affected by urbanisation and relatively high money incomes – in that sense the Carpenter objective of a completely urbanised labour force, divorced from the land, has proved to have been too simple, too much a product of ideas based on conditions in older industrial countries. And the developing shortage of land will probably increase its attractiveness to urbanised workers and perhaps even increase their relative ability to afford it.

Most obviously, the gap between urban wages and conditions and the real income of smallholder farming has clearly grown. The real income of smallholders has perhaps become even more difficult to measure in recent years – the evaluation of 'subsistence', the possibility of cash sales in local markets, and of part-time wage earning, the incidence of cash flows from relatives in wage employment, the valuation of land itself. But the general widening of the gap has not been in doubt. The Salaries Commission concluded (Report p. 22): 'between 1960 and the end of 1965 the average income of African wage-earners increased by 80 per cent, or more than three times the rate of increase of gross domestic product. During this period, the average income of small farmers increased by about 20 per cent, or *less* than the growth of gross domestic product'. As it also says, small farmers have much less access to social services, schools, hospitals, and so on.

Evidence suggests that with maintenance of profitable prices and development of better marketing facilities, etc., many smallholders could raise productivity, output and incomes relatively easily. But in the short run it seems probable that population pressure on land combined with increases of incomes in towns – unless these are restrained rather sharply – will tend to increase the gap. So, though there has been an increasing stabilisation of the urban labour force, to which higher wages and conditions, development of skills, and also the contraction of employment opportunities since the late 1950s, have all contributed, so that labour turnover in large firms in the Nairobi area is now very low indeed, rural-urban migration of the traditional kind still seems to be an important aspect of the life of both the towns and the rural areas, and it may even increase if the 'school-leaver' problem continues to rise. This of course raises the whole question of the strategy of economic development. In Kenya the need to develop large and smallscale (mainly settlement) agriculture bulked largely in economic planning both before and after Independence; realisation of the need to concentrate even more on general development in the rural areas has grown recently, and is likely to be an important influence in further planning.

IV
The organisation of industrial relations

One of the major issues of the 1960s, with the coming of Independence and of comprehensive planning for rapid development, has been the rôle that government should play in the labour market. It has been an important question in the area of industrial relations.

The organisation of industrial relations at national, industry and enterprise levels – for all save the smallest enterprises, at any rate – developed largely on the basis of the KFL/FKE agreements of 1957–8. These agreed on the desirability of collective bargaining and on its basic structure, objectives and methods. The agreements certainly did not prevent the emergence of quite serious industrial disputes, but, just as certainly, they facilitated the development of 'normal' working relationships in industries and firms, which, of course, got far less publicity than did stoppages but were real and important achievements. In 1961 KFL and FKE formed a National Joint Consultative Council, to which issues which seemed likely to lead to strikes or lockouts might be referred voluntarily by the parties concerned for rapid advice. Joint Industrial Councils spread in industries, as did other negotiating bodies. By the end of 1962 there were 52 employees' unions registered, and 19 employers' – in law these were also treated as unions.

In 1962 the Industrial Relations Charter was drawn up by KFL, FKE, and the Ministry of Labour. This was a tripartite statement of intent and guide to both sides of industry. It outlined agreed responsibilities of each side in industrial relations, with a model Recognition Agreement, and outlined principles governing negotiations so as to minimize disputes and the resort to stoppages, and principles which should guide both sides in questions of redundancy – by then a major preoccupation with several unions. It encouraged joint consultation at plant level. It provided for joint KFL/FKE Disputes Commissions to which voluntary reference might be made without prejudice to the existing collective bargaining system and the

Ministry of Labour's system of conciliation and arbitration. This 'tripartite' approach has been important since then, and the charter itself, which received quite wide publicity in several other countries, had very considerable influence in Kenya. It provided some guidance to relatively inexperienced unions and employers, including incoming subsidiaries of foreign groups; along with advice from FKE it probably encouraged some employers to more rapid acceptance of collective bargaining with national unions than would otherwise have been the case. The model Recognition Agreement in particular became almost standard procedure, and, once this was agreed, negotiation of agreements on wages and conditions – for the most part very comprehensive – also tended to become standardised among employers' associations and individual firms which, increasingly, affiliated to the FKE.

In 1962 also, the desirability of a 'high wage economy' was reasserted by the Ministers of Labour of the three East African countries: a principle to which KFL, FKE and the Ministry of Labour subscribed – though no doubt their interpretation of what it meant in detail and in the pace at which wages should rise varied!

However, in 1962 to 1965 the national industrial relations scene became very complex and confused. This was partly because of the very variable viability and competence of individual unions, particularly in the agricultural sector. KFL's policy was to strengthen unions and make better use of scarce resources of administrative and negotiating ability and finance by encouraging amalgamations. In this they sometimes clashed with employers' groups, especially in agriculture; one major result, in 1963, was the formation of the Kenya Plantation and Agricultural Workers Union, which replaced four smaller unions none of which had proved very viable; only the Sugar Plantation Workers' Union remained separate.

Though the National Joint Consultative Council functioned effectively in many cases, both before and after Independence there were many strikes for both political and more narrowly 'professional' reasons (it was hard to distinguish these in practice, at least from the unions' point of view); many were initiated not by the unions as such but by individual shop steward and workers with grievances. Many disputes had to go to arbitration or boards of inquiry. The union movement itself split in 1964, partly over the issue of KFL's affiliation to ICFTU, partly, perhaps, simply because of clashes of personalities among the small number of outstanding union leaders, partly over the desire of some for a monolithic union of the kind that had been introduced in Tanzania rather than KFL's federal structure and policy of encouraging amalgamations. In April 1964 the radical leaders of three relatively powerful unions – the Mombasa

Dockers, the Railway African Union and the Kenya Petroleum Oil Workers' Union – were expelled from KFL, and proceeded to establish a rival organisation based on their unions and trying to get support from members of other unions which were still affiliated to KFL. In 1965 the Kenya African Workers' Congress was registered.

This split was one reason for several disputes and stoppages; it created widespread uncertainty for employers and workers alike. In February 1964 the Tripartite Agreement for the Immediate Relief of Unemployment had been negotiated. By it, for the period of twelve months, the public sector undertook to take on 15 per cent more workers than their existing labour force, and private employers 10 per cent more; there was to be no redundancy, no dismissals except in accordance with collective agreements, or with the agreement of a tripartite committee and if workers were dismissed or left employment, they were to be replaced. In return KFL for the unions agreed that there would be a wage pause during the course of the agreement and no strikes; FKE for the employers agreed that there would be no lockouts, and government agreed that it would establish an Industrial Court for voluntary arbitration, and draw up and publish a 'wages policy'. But in fact, during the fourteen months of the agreement, the number of disputes and stoppages actually rose, and when it ended in 1965 a backlog of wage claims and other issues seemed likely to lead to widespread unrest once more.

In 1964 the Industrial Court was established, and almost at once became a major factor in the collective bargaining system and industrial relations generally. In 1965 the government intervened much more positively. First, the Trade Disputes Act of 1965 was passed. Its main aim was to ensure that unions and employers actually adhered to and fully utilised agreed procedures for handling disputes. It required that disputes be referred to the Ministry of Labour and set up a tripartite committee to advise the Minister of Labour on action to be taken about these disputes. It gave the Minister power to declare actual or threatened stoppages illegal if he felt that negotiating procedures had not been fully used. It re-established the Industrial Court (with no break in continuity) and provided that in the case of a widened range of 'essential services' (including fuel, petrol, power and lighting, railways and the port and harbour services in Mombasa) disputes could be referred compulsorily to the Court; whereas the Court's decisions in other cases had no legal standing except that, if accepted by both sides, they became implied terms of contract subject to the law covering contract, its awards in the case of references which concerned essential services were to be binding on the parties. The Minister was also given power to declare 'sympathetic' strikes and lockouts illegal. Finally the Act provided for the 'check-off' as a method of collecting union dues.

Later in 1965 both KFL (which had meantime disaffiliated from ICFTU) and the new KAWC were brought to an end. In their place the government establish one central organisation, COTU, to which all unions were affiliated and in which the government had representation on the executive committee (as had all unions) and senior officials were to be appointed by the President of the country from nominees put forward by the executive committee. 15 per cent of 'check-off' dues were to go to COTU.

The 1965 Act, the Tripartite Committee, the Industrial Court, and the imposition of at least nominal unity in the union movement, together perhaps with growing realisation of the country's employment and other economic problems, led to a considerable reduction in the number of stoppages. The Minister has used his power to declare actual or threatened strikes illegal relatively rarely: in 1966 on seventeen occasions (the number of reported disputes in that year was 155) in only one of which – a strike by the Kenya National Union of Teachers towards the end of the year – did his action arouse controversy, though clearly the question of whether 'existing machinery' has been fully utilised is itself a matter of judgment in some disputes. (One trend which was not foreseen by the framers of the 1965 Act was a growing use of 'go-slows' in preference to strikes; in law these are not regarded as strikes.) Clearly, however, the Minister's powers of intervention under the Act are very considerable.

A.R.PREST

The Finances of Small Countries

I

In discussing this subject the first things to do are to specify the problem and to outline its general importance. Small countries can be defined in a variety of different ways but I shall concentrate here on small countries defined in terms of population as distinct from income or area. Obviously, the dividing line between small and large populations is arbitrary, but what I have in mind is something of the order of two and a half million people or so – roughly the size of a number of major urban areas in Western countries (e.g. Manchester, Birmingham, Boston). Naturally, the precise conclusions will differ if other arbitrary dividing lines are taken and this must be borne in mind throughout. Another point is the implicit assumption about the density of population per square mile. We might think in terms of countries having small populations but with an average density of population per square mile or a density which is less or greater than that found in the world at large. Our principal emphasis will in fact be on small countries with an average density of population, but we shall cast one or two glances at the more particular problems of those which are sparsely or densely populated as well.

One other point which will recur on a number of occasions should be made now. This is simply that if one is comparing small countries with larger ones, then one obviously has to watch for other reasons which might vitiate any comparisons. It is no good, for instance, comparing countries with small and large populations if they differ vastly in a variety of respects such as income per capita or geographical location in the world, or, for that matter, in the basic structure of their economic systems. By the latter, I mean simply that comparisons between small and big countries where the small one was run on more or less capitalist lines and the large one was run on Soviet-type lines would clearly not be very meaningful.

We now say something about the importance of this subject. In a sense, one need not look further than the UK in 1968 to justify this paper. With the movements for Home Rule or Independence in Scotland, Wales, etc., the problems we discuss in this paper obviously do concern us very closely in this country. However, to broaden the analysis, one can simply look at the United Nations Statistical Yearbook.[1] If one counts the number of countries for which population data are given, one finds that out of 139 independent countries, there are 37 with a population of less than $2\frac{1}{2}$ million; and out of 57 non-self-governing territories there are 52 with a population of less than $2\frac{1}{2}$ million. So if one adds these two groups together one has a total of 89 countries out of 196 with populations of less than $2\frac{1}{2}$ million. The reaction to such figures might be that countries cannot be simply enumerated one by one in this way, and that one must give greater weighting to countries which exercise large influence in the world, by virtue of their population, income, area, etc. However, it should be remembered that in the eyes of the United Nations, even if not those of the Lord, all animals are equal, and each independent country, at any rate, does have a single vote and no one country has more than that. We should also remember the talk about the pressure being exercised by the 77 developing countries at the second UNCTAD meeting in Delhi. Not all these 77 countries are in the small population class, of course, but nevertheless a substantial fraction is.

It might be argued that, even though there is a large number of small countries in the world today nevertheless it is likely to diminish rapidly in the future. I see no evidence whatever for a proposition of this sort, given the background of nationalistic feeling which one finds anywhere and everywhere in the world. Consider, for instance, how the number of countries might be reduced. First of all, there might be a voluntary merger, say, in the form of a federation. But the experience of federally united countries in recent years hardly gives one much reason for thinking that this development is going to be important in the near future. After all, the Federation of the West Indies and the Central African Federation both broke up in the early sixties; the union of Singapore and Malaysia was short-lived; the future of the East African Federation is by no means certain; and the Federation of Nigeria has tended to become looser over the years with the transition from three to four Regions and, more recently, to twelve States. So it would not seem that this development is very likely. Alternatively, one might argue that the number of small countries would be reduced through a compulsory merger, i.e. through conquest or absorption. This could certainly happen but, once again, given the watching presence of international agencies and the like, one would have thought that this was a much less likely development than in the nineteenth century. So I should be surprised if this were to be an important phenomenon in the future. Thirdly, one might imagine that some countries could disappear simply by becoming uninhabited, say, in the way in which islands in the Outer Hebrides have become uninhabited during this century. Once again, one must judge this to be an unlikely development, given the pattern of world immigration laws.

I am therefore taking the view that we have a lot of small countries in the world today, and that we are likely to go on having a lot in the future. It is perfectly true that there have always been a number of small principalities, such as Monaco and Andorra in Europe, but some of the developments of the post-war world such as the breaking of colonial ties and the intense nationalistic fervour of many new countries make it likely that this phenomenon will be much more widespread in the future than it has been in the past.

It may be that after due exploration we shall find that the fact of smallness, as measured by population, is not a major issue for the finance of government either on the revenue or the expenditure side, but *prima facie* it seems a worthwhile exercise to enquire whether it is or not.

II

In this section I propose to look at some of the *a priori* arguments which might lead one to think that small countries would have a different financial set-up or a different set of financial issues to face compared to large countries. I do wish to emphasise that at this stage the argument is essentially that of the traditional armchair theorist, and we shall not become involved in any detailed empirical evidence until we reach the next section.

It may be useful, first of all, to try to deduce what some of the general economic characteristics of small countries are likely to be compared to large countries. Subsequently, we can consider in more detail the likely impact on the expenditure and revenue sides of government.

If we are to discourse on the general economic characteristics of small countries, one clearly has to specify some relevant alternative set of political arrangements. In this context, the comparison is often made between a small country and a big one, notwithstanding the fact that the two are logically bound to differ from one another in respect of either land area or density of population – thereby tending to vitiate the comparison in one way[2] or another. It would seem more sensible to make a comparison between the characteristics of a number of small countries all independent of one another and, on the other hand, the characteristics of a united country embracing all the small ones. The precise form of the political organization of the united country can reasonably be a matter of opinion, but perhaps it is most plausible to assume that it would be a loose kind of federation. This is, after all, the most likely alternative to having a series of independent states. The really important proposition is that for some purposes one wants to compare the characteristics of all the small countries taken together with those of the larger geographical area which forms the federation. It may be a reasonable simplification at some points to select one of the small countries (a 'representative country') to compare with the federal area, but the basic model must surely be that of comparing the whole congeries of small countries with the larger one. One could clearly think of other alternatives, e.g. a large area splitting up into a slightly less large one and another very small unit and then compare the characteristics of the two new units with the old one. But we shall not take that particular course of reasoning here.

Further clarification is also needed about the precise basis of comparison between the federated and the de-federated positions. For some purposes, it will be sufficient to make the comparison on a simple before and after basis. But for other purposes we shall need to envisage how the economy might have developed over time if federation had continued relatively to the course of events in the various units after de-federation.[3] We shall endeavour to make the precise basis of comparison clear in each case as we go along. The first point of comparison between the federated and the de-federated positions is that, almost by definition, the volume of international trade relatively to internal trade will increase. Trade flows between the units which took place in the days of the federation were regarded as internal flows; now they must be regarded as international flows. So unless there is a very marked reduction in the amount of trade between the small units, taken all together, and the rest of the world, or unless there is a large reduction in the amount of trade flows between the units – or some combination of both these reductions – it must follow that the volume of international trade will increase. Another important consequence also follows de-federation. Whereas a federation may well embrace a variety of different specializations, this is far less likely for each individual unit. It follows from this that the likelihood of income fluctuation over time is much greater for the representative small country than for the federation as a whole.

The exact effects on the volume and pattern of international trade will obviously be dependent on the changes in tariffs and other protective devices (as well as any in relative costs, incomes, taxes etc.) which come about as a result of the breaking up of the federation. There is no fundamental reason why a federation should be associated with free trade between the units (e.g., the West Indies Federation of the late 1950s.); and there is no basic reason why trade between units which have de-federated should be subject to protective devices of any kind. Nevertheless, it seems a reasonable assumption that the impediments to trade between the units are likely to be greater after the break-up of federation. There may also be upward changes in respect of tariffs, etc., between this group of countries and the rest of the world, for reasons we shall come to in a moment.

On the plausible assumption that impediments to trade between the units are likely to be greater once de-federation has taken place, it would seem reasonable to hypothesise that the potentialities for the growth of manufacturing industry will be less than before. Purely on the grounds that the advantages of economies of scale are more likely to be fully reaped if one has a large domestic market than if one has to battle for external outlets defederation will result in a larger volume of imported manufactures from the rest of the world and less domestic production than would otherwise have been the case. [4] The corollary is therefore that one may find a faster rate of growth of services, and perhaps of agriculture, and so on, after de-federation, as the volume of employment in secondary activity will grow more slowly. To some extent, this proposition works in the opposite direction to that mentioned above, in that, if the volume of manufacturing production grows more slowly there will tend to be less manufacturing trade flows between the units after de-federation than would otherwise have been the case; unless this is compensated by larger flows of other products, there will therefore tend to be comparatively smaller trade flows *in toto* between the units. This, of course, does not controvert the general conclusion that the total amount of international trade will be greater after de-federation than before.

There may be many influences other than tariff changes, affecting the volume of trade between the units. For instance, if de-federation is accompanied by the growth or resuscitation of individual languages in the different units in substitution for some *lingua franca*, this might, in due course, lead to cultural differences and a reduction in the rate of increase of trade flows, quite apart from that due to any tariff barriers.

Given the general conclusion about a lower rate of growth of manufacturing industry in a situation of defederation, it is likely that the growth of the corporate sector of the economy will also be less, as this tends to be associated more with manufacturing than with other activities such as tourism, services or agriculture.

Another characteristic of de-federated units is that one is then more likely to find a situation in which one or two firms are very powerful, relatively, to the government. It could, of course, be the case that even in a federation a particular foreign firm, say, might play a part in every territory and therefore its overall size, relative to that of the federal government, would be large. But it is much more likely that such foreign firms will be differentially important in the various units, and so the likelihood of their having positions of dominance is greater when one has a collection of small countries rather than a single federation. What I have in mind here is the dominance of particular firms such as the United Fruit Company in the banana republics of Central America. Quite apart from the general effects on the degree of competition, this will obviously have important repercussions on such matters as the government's bargaining power in respect of taxation, import or export prices, wages legislation and so on.

Another likely development is that the collectivity of small countries may be able to extract more in aid from Western countries than one federally organized area. It has become increasingly clear in recent years that aid does not increase proportionately to size of population, and so it would therefore follow that a number of small countries speaking with a number of different voices may be able to extract more *in toto* than would be the case with one single large organization.[5] So even if the trade developments imply a reduction in the rate of increase of income per head, they may be partly or wholly compensated by increases in external aid. On the other hand, there are factors working for more inequality of income distribution between countries. There is no longer a federal government to reduce income disparities between units by suitable revenue or expenditure policies[6]; and in so far as movements of capital and labour are more likely to be inhibited by tax laws or other barriers if a number of countries de-federate, inequality will be greater still. This would tend to be the case, for instance, even if restrictions on labour movements principally affected seasonal workers rather than long term permanent immigrants.

The precise result of these various changes on the growth of income per head in the de-federated case is not easy to predict. If one thinks that the disadvantages of more impediments to trade, of a slower rate of industrialization, and of the reduced rate of adoption of a corporate form of enterprise, etc., are important, one is likely to conclude that growth will be slower. But there are clearly many imponderables in reaching an exact conclusion and we do not pretend to reach one here. What would seem to be much clearer is that fluctuations of income over time will be greater, whatever the precise statistical technique of measuring them, as a result of greater specialisation among the independent units than would have been the case in the federation as a whole.

After this general review, we now look at the more specific characteristics of de-federation which concern us here. First of all, what can be said about the government expenditure side ? There are a number of points which immediately spring to mind. If one is contrasting a unitary government system for the whole area with a number of independent governments, the initial presumption is that one will have more in the way of government administrative expenses in the latter case. If, on the other hand, the comparison is between a federal system and independence the answer is not so clear, as one will in that case be eliminating one layer of government; though the savings in costs may be small if all the ex-federal employees have to be found new government jobs. Another general point is that there is likely to be greater contact and greater cohesion between the government and its population. This 'grass roots' argument could work in either of two directions. First, it is likely that pressures on governments to spend will be greater when the bulk of the population is just round the corner, so to speak. On the other hand, it can also be argued that with such a local government type of arrangement there is more likely to be willingness to pay on the part of the population for these expenditures. Which, on balance, of these two influences will predominate, it is impossible to say. The subject of economies of scale in government administration was explored by Professor Robinson at some length in a paper at an International Economics Association Conference[7] and I do not wish to add much to this here. He came to the general conclusion that although there are some obvious losses in small countries, especially small poor countries, e.g. the overheads of running a Central Bank or keeping foreign exchange reserves, or financing a University, or the maintenance of embassies and consulates abroad, there are also other economies such as the greater co-ordination and flexibility of governments and so on. One particular point might be noted: in so far as there are potential losses due to the inability to employ their own specialists, small governments can by-pass such difficulties in much the same way as small firms can by-pass the difficulties of not being able to have a large number of specialists on their payrolls. The standard procedure for small firms is to use a specialist agency. In just the same way small countries can belong to a Common Services Organization (e.g. East Africa) or have an Associated States status, as in the West Indies; or they can call in international consultants to help them, say, appraise investment proposals involving government assistance; or they can join a defence alliance in order to economise on costs of military expenditures. Indeed, one can also argue that in so far as the ethnic cohesion of small countries is likely to be larger than that of large countries, this is, in turn, likely to mean less demands for policing than would otherwise be the case. One should not overdo this latter point in that savings in police might be offset by increases in expenditure on the Armed Forces, but it is simply an example of the sort of issue which arises.

In his investigation, Professor Robinson looked into these matters of economies of scale in relation to administration, defence, economic services and social services, and came to the general conclusion that a small country (a 'representative small country' in our model) was not likely to be at any serious disadvantage. His argument was essentially that the number of devices available to avoid the diseconomies of small size is sufficiently large for this conclusion to hold over a wide range of country sizes ranging upwards from a relatively low level.

We now turn to the revenue characteristics which one may expect to find on *a priori* grounds in a representative small country. The first point is the ratio of total tax revenue to national income. Are there any grounds for thinking that it may tend to be smaller or larger than in countries with larger populations? It is not easy to see any clearcut answer to this question. The grounds on which governments may intervene either in the sense of buying goods and services or in that of making larger amounts of transfer payments or in that of taking over the running of various sectors of the economy are multifarious, and there are no very strong reasons why one should find such a tremendous difference between small and large countries in this respect. One reason which may be important in some circumstances should be mentioned. The pressure on government to take over the running of public utilities and the like may be greater in a small country than in a large country where the availability of indigenous private enterprise for such purposes may be more likely. It seems a fair assumption to say that the likelihood of foreign companies or enterprises being allowed such concessions is fairly limited – unlike the nineteenth-century position – and so that possibility need not detain us too much. But this point apart, there are no obvious *a priori* reasons why one should expect the overall ratio to differ significantly between countries of different population sizes.

What does seem much more certain is that fluctuations in revenue will be greater from one year to another as a result of the greater fluctuations in GNP which we have already postulated. Although tax rates can be adjusted downwards when, say, incomes from exporting a particular crop rise, in practice adjustments may not be well-timed; and in the reverse case when incomes fall, it may be quite impracticable to raise tax rates sufficiently to stabilise revenues.

This brings us to the subject of direct taxes, whether on individuals or on corporations. There are several points which are relevant here. The first is that on the basis of our arguments about manufacturing industry and the corporate sector, one is likely to have a larger agricultural and services sector and a larger number of small firms or

L

partnerships, sole traders, etc., than would otherwise have been the case. For these sorts of reasons then, one must be prepared to face the facts that company income taxes will yield less revenue and personal income tax may be relatively more difficult to levy in the circumstances of small countries.

There are also some other points to note in respect of the operation of direct taxes. The first is that it is a well-known feature of many developing countries that they grant concessions to various enterprises which are often, though not necessarily, expatriate, in the form of tax holidays, accelerated depreciation and so on. If one has a large number of small countries competing with one another in these respects, one is likely to find that the average degree of concession may well be greater than if the small countries were organized in the form of one single federal unit. Of course, this may not be so. If there are 90 countries in the world offering concessions, and the choice between federation and de-federation only concerns two of them, one would not expect this to have much effect on the pattern of concessions. But it clearly remains a possibility. Whether it would have any substantial effect in reducing the amount of foreign investment is another issue requiring detailed analysis which would take us rather beyond the scope of our analysis here. The second point is that in a situation where one does have de-federation on the lines envisaged, the chances are that a series of separate income tax systems will be introduced in these countries and over time they will begin to diverge in various minor, or even major, respects. Once this happens, the opportunities for tax avoidance and evasion tend to multiply. Companies locate their headquarter offices and arrange the organisation of their subsidiaries so as to minimise total tax outgoings; similarly, individuals, or at any rate those who are substantial taxpayers, will also arrange affairs to their own advantage. The old motto attributed to the residents on the borders between Northern and Southern Ireland ('Divided we stand; united we fall') has direct relevance here. Finally, it is worth observing that in the most successful federations – USA, Canada, Australia, for instance – there has been an increasing tendency over time for the central government to play a larger role in the assessment and collection of income tax. In Canada, for instance, the Dominion Government now collects personal income tax on behalf of all Provinces except Quebec and corporation tax on behalf of all except Quebec and Ontario – the two most populous, it might be noted. This experience does suggest that there are good reasons – political, as well as administrative and economic – for thinking that there are advantages in operating one large income tax system rather than a series of small ones.

What can be said about indirect taxes ? The first observation is that if international trade flows are absolutely more important after de-federation, this is likely to be a help rather than a hindrance in tax collection. Import and export taxes are customarily more easily levied than excise or sales taxes in developing countries.

On the other hand, foreign elasticities of supply to and demand for the products of any one small country will be greater than with a large one, and so the possibility of shifting the burden of such taxes to foreigners will be less. Furthermore, we have argued that a slower rate of growth of the manufacturing sector in the defederated case is likely to mean that agriculture will remain more important than it otherwise would have done. So fluctuations in tax revenues consequent on variations in agricultural output and/or prices will continue to be a major feature of tax systems.

We have made the point that government running of public utilities is virtually inevitable in small countries. There is a good deal of evidence to show that such operations usually tend to be a drain on general revenues rather than a support for them. So whatever the arguments for such operating losses in terms of economic efficiency or income distribution, we must expect them to add to budgetary strain.

A variety of other developments is likely. Although, as we saw above, the total amount of aid to the collectivity of small countries is likely to exceed that to the large one, the reverse is likely to be the case in respect of international borrowing terms. One would think, on *a priori* grounds, that the credit rating of a large country would be greater and so the terms of international borrowing less onerous.

One characteristic feature of many federal constitutions is the need to have regular fiscal reviews to share out revenues between the constituent countries. Although these reviews are settled amicably enough in some cases, in others they are the occasion for bitter and protracted bickering. At least this occasion for animosity would disappear if de-federation took place. Finally, it may be worth observing that the EEC is proposing that most of the taxes in the Community should in due course be harmonised. As the Community consists of a number of very different sized countries this suggests that the disadvantages of small size cannot be overwhelming for any tax; or that at least, if they are great for one tax, they are counterbalanced by opposing advantages for others.

III

At the risk of a charge of casual empiricism, we must confine ourselves to statistical evidence on a selected number of the points enumerated in our analysis. Moreover, our approach will often have

to be an oblique one. It is also recognised that the statistical techniques used are very simple; more powerful ones could yield different
answers.

We shall, in fact look at the position of small countries compared
to a large one, under the following general headings, selecting particular points in each case:

1 Overall tax/GNP ratio
2 Government revenue composition
3 Government revenue collection efficiency
4 Government expenditure composition
5 Government expenditure efficiency

1. Overall tax/GNP ratio

There have been a number of attempts in recent years to explain
overall tax/GNP ratios for different countries. [8] For our purposes the
most useful is that by Lotz and Morss. Essentially, they tabulate the
tax/GNP ratio for 52 developing countries, ranking countries according to the size of the ratio. Subsequently, using regressions, they
standardize the tax/GNP ratio correcting, first, for differences in *per
capita* income and, second, for differences in both *per capita* income
and 'openness' (defined as the ratio of imports plus exports to GNP).
The last ratio is considered to be a more reasonable indication of
'tax effort' on the grounds that one would expect tax/income ratios to
differ between countries with differing *per capita* incomes or degrees
of openness.

If one divides the 52 countries into large and small, one can then
classify the Lotz and Morss findings as shown in table 1. (We start
with a dividing line of $2\frac{1}{2}$m population in part A; but also try out
another of 5m in part B, to see how sensitive the results are to any
such change.)

There must clearly be many statistical reservations about any such
results, e.g. the inevitable weakness of the data, and the unsatisfactory nature of some of these particular regression equations. But,
for what they are worth, the results seem to show that after standardisation on both counts, [9] small countries are not able to achieve high
tax/GNP ratios as easily as large ones, e.g. with the $2\frac{1}{2}$ million dividing
line, 6 out of the 8 small countries are in the low bracket compared
with only 11 of the 44 large; and with the 5 million dividing line
10 out of 18 small are in this category and only 7 out of 34 large.
The differential effects of income per head and openness are such as
to obscure this conclusion if one simply takes the crude tax/GNP
ratios.

So it would appear that there is some evidence to show that
relatively more small countries than large are likely to be in the low

TABLE 1   Tax/GNP ratios for 52 countries

	High ratio bracket		Average ratio bracket		Low ratio bracket	
	Small	*Large*	*Small*	*Large*	*Small*	*Large*
Part A						
Tax/GNP ratio	0	12	6	17	2	15
Ratio adjusted for *per capita* income	1	11	3	20	4	13
Ratio adjusted for *per capita* income and openness	0	12	2	21	6	11
Part B						
Tax/GNP ratio	1	11	10	13	7	12
Ratio adjusted for *per capita* income	2	10	7	16	9	8
Ratio adjusted for *per capita* income and openness	4	8	4	19	10	7

Number of countries in:

Source: Lotz & Morss, *op. cit.*
Note: Total number in each high, average and low bracket is the same as that given in Table 4, Lotz & Morss, *op. cit.*

'tax effort' category. This could be due either to a voluntary preference for relatively lower levels of public expenditure or to sheer
inability to raise the same proportion of income in taxation. A study
of the variations in revenue/expenditure ratios between countries
might throw some light on this. But such an exercise must remain
for the future.

2. Government revenue composition

We concluded earlier that one might expect small countries to raise
a relatively larger proportion of their indirect taxes from import and
export duties. The only data by which we can test this proposition
are those in the *U.N. Statistical Yearbook*[10] and these may very well
not fit the particular circumstances of our model. For what they are
worth, we find that out of 26 developing countries, there are 11 with
populations of less than 5m[11] and 15 with population in excess. The

unweighted mean ratio of import and export to total indirect taxes
for the former is 60 per cent and for the latter 58 per cent. So on this
basis, one clearly cannot conclude that there is any significant
difference between small and large countries. However, all the
reasons why the 11 may differ from the 15 in other respects (e.g.
geography and history) must be remembered.[13]

3. Government revenue collection efficiency

Data are usually given in tax departments' reports about costs of
collection. Such figures only refer to officially incurred costs; and
international comparisons are likely to be hazardous. But, in one
respect at least, there is a justification for making such comparisons.
In so far as costs of collection are kept low at the expense of gathering less revenue, there will automatically be some degree of standardization for quality of performance if we compare ratios of collection
costs to revenue intake.

Examination of income tax department reports for a number of
countries did not in fact suggest that variations in the collection/
revenue ratio are clearly associated with size. One finds, for instance,
that in three countries – Jamaica, Barbados, Mauritius – with similar
systems inherited from British Colonial days – that the ratios were
respectively 1 per cent, 0·9 per cent and 1·8 per cent in recent years.
Mauritius is smaller than Jamaica but has a higher ratio; Barbados
is smaller than Jamaica but has a lower ratio. And, if it means
anything to compare with the figure in an entirely different country,
the UK, the 1965–66 figure there was 1·4 per cent. So it does not look
as if one is going to find major differences between countries in
pursuing this line of investigation.

Some miscellaneous evidence on this topic is to be found in
Nigeria. In an investigation of income taxation in the old Western
Region of Nigeria, Orewa[14] found that the larger the district the
greater the degree of income tax evasion. For instance, in Ibadan
district he estimated that in 1957–8 only 95,000 were paying tax out
of a possible 193,000; whereas in Iwo there were some 18,000 actual
taxpayers out of a potential 19,000. Orewa attributed these very
marked differences to the much greater personal contacts between
first, tax rate assessors and collectors, and second, rate assessors and
taxpayers in small communities. A further reason was that traders
were more likely to be mobile and difficult to catch than rural
workers; and the proportion of traders was likely to be greater in
large urban areas. It must be remembered, however, that these findings relate to an income tax system with a substantial element of poll
taxation in it.

More generally, Nigeria provides a good example of the problems of running a variety of income tax systems instead of a single one for the whole country.[15] Adedeji argued in 1965[16] that a single Federal personal income tax system would have very considerable advantages over the five income tax systems then existing in terms of cheaper administration, more conformity of administrative practice, less evasion and so on. Given the more recent division of the country into twelve states, instead of four Regions, this argument is surely overwhelmingly right, though the signs at the time of writing seem to point to the likelihood of at least 13 income tax systems in the country.

4. Government expenditure composition

It does not seem possible to deduce much from data on relative amounts spent under different heads. First, despite the very valuable work done by the UN in producing comparable data for a number of countries[17] the problems of non-uniform classifications are still formidable. Second, and more fundamental, even if we can ignore this point, it is difficult to see what conclusions can be drawn from simple comparisons of expenditure patterns in large and small countries. It may be that, say, the ratio of education to total expenditure is higher in a smaller country; this could be due to inescapable diseconomies of small size but it could also simply reflect relative income levels or relative preferences on the part of voters or their representatives. The ratio of defence to total expenditure is likely to depend on the hostility of neighbours or the possibilities of entering into alliances, just as much as, if not more than, on the size of population. Expenditure on roads is likely to be a function of density of population. Unless one can eliminate all these reasons for non-comparability, expenditure composition data will not be very illuminating.

5. Government expenditure efficiency

Inter-country comparisons of efficiency under different spending heads are useless unless allowances can somehow be made for such other variables as differences in quality of services provided. I know no means of doing this on an international basis. But comparisons between local authorities within a given country may shed some light, even if very obliquely, on the problem.

In the UK, there are various sources from which one can build up some impressions – in this context, a more appropriate word than conclusions. A few years ago the Royal Commission on Local Government in Greater London came to the conclusion that there was no optimum size of local authority in economic terms.[18] The Rural District Councils Associations recently gave evidence to the

Royal Commission on Local Government in England and Wales.[19]
Chapter VI of this document made an analysis of costs of administration incurred by local authorities in providing a standard list of
services. Although there was a small tendency for costs per head of
population to fall with the size of the authority (e.g., for small
county boroughs the figure was about £1·7 per head; for large ones
it was £1·6) the general conclusion was that there were no important
diseconomies of small size within the ranges covered (roughly,
30,000–400,000 population). The pertinent point was made that re-
organisation of functions, boundaries, etc., is a much more likely
cause of cost increases than the small size of authorities.[20]

Detailed figures are published each year by the Institution of
Municipal Treasurers and Accountants for local authority expenditure in England and Wales. As an experiment, the data on police
expenditure for the different county boroughs[21] were analysed. A
rough correction for quality of service was made by comparing
groups of towns for which there was a very similar ratio of population to policemen. Given this element of standardisation, it was then
possible to compare police expenditure per head of population
between towns. The result was that there was no systematic variation
with size and no evidence to suggest that small authorities, at any
rate within the range covered (minimum size 65,000) suffered
relatively to larger ones. Too much should not be read into these
figures: the standardization was very crude (e.g., crime rates may
differ considerably between towns even if they have the same number
of policemen per thousand population), the statistical techniques
used were rough and ready and immediate application to countries
with entirely different backgrounds, levels of income and so on
would be foolhardy. The experiment was simply a very crude one
which needs to be repeated on a much larger scale and refined
pattern.

As another example of intra-country comparisons of expenditure
efficiency, we may take Kiesling's investigation into education expenditure in New York State.[22] In a multiple regression analysis of
educational performance with respect to pupil intelligence, school
district, size, etc., in 97 school districts, he was not able to find any
evidence of economies of scale with respect to size, as measured by
average daily attendance at all schools in the district. If anything
there was a hint of diseconomies of scale.

It may be worth remarking that in countries as different as the UK
and Australia, grants from the Central Government to lower tiers
have for many years given extra weight to those areas with low
population densities, on the grounds that they had special burdens
to bear in respect of such items as road maintenance, school upkeep,

etc. So even though there is not much evidence of differences in expenditure performance between a representative small population and a large one,[23] there are grounds for distinguishing those small sized units which are lightly populated.

But it must be strongly stressed that conclusions drawn from local authorities in relatively advanced countries cannot be applied across the board to the much less developed countries we have in mind in this paper. Such conclusions are no more than a start to any proper statistical investigation.

How can we summarise these very scattered and very variegated pieces of empirical evidence ? There is some evidence to show that small countries make smaller 'tax efforts' than large ones, once allowances have been made for differences in income per head and in openness of the economy. But it is difficult to say exactly what interpretation should be placed on this result. As far as government revenue goes, there does not seem to be much in the proposition that small countries are likely to raise a larger fraction of their indirect taxes from import and export duties; but possibly rather more in the fear that a multiple system of income taxes leads to difficulties. On the expenditure side, comparisons of relative amounts spent under different headings are not likely to be very meaningful; and such evidence as there is on expenditure efficiency does not suggest that small countries necessarily suffer in this respect.

A great deal more work needs to be done before any conclusions can be advanced with any confidence of any sort. But at this stage the very tentative impression must be that whatever the larger political and economic consequences of de-federation (or of any alternative political machinery by which small countries are created) there is no overwhelming evidence of disastrous results necessarily following in the public finance field.

Notes and references
1 *U.N. Statistical Yearbook* 1966 (New York 1967).
2 E.g. a greater land area is likely to mean greater opportunities for trade.
3 The advantage of assuming a federation initially, and then tracing the consequences of de-federation rather than the other way round is that this is slightly more complex. One then has to think, for instance, about the disbanding of the federal government or the financial consequences if the former federal employees have to be absorbed in the new government structure.
4 Intensified policies of import substitution may prevent the absolute volume of output and/or employment in manufacturing from declining but it seems reasonable to assume that the rate of increase will nonetheless be smaller than it otherwise would have been.
5 cf. I.M.D.Little and J.M.Clifford *International Aid* (London 1965) p. 94 n.1 for corroboration and also for a reference to an unpublished econometric analysis by A.Strout.

6 In so far as governments tend to concentrate expenditure (e.g. hospitals) on capital cities, de-federation and an increase in relative importance of hitherto minor capitals might make for less rather than more inequality on the spending side.

7 E.A.G.Robinson 'The Size of Nations and the Cost of Administration'. In E.A.G.Robinson (ed.) *The Economic Consequences of the Size of Nations* (London 1960) ch. 14.

8 See e.g. A.M.Martin and W.A.Lewis 'Patterns of Public Revenue and Expenditure' *The Manchester School* September 1956; J.G.Williamson 'Public Expenditure and Revenue: An International Comparison; *Manchester School* January 1961; Harley H. Hinrichs *A General Theory of Tax Structure Change During Economic Development* (Cambridge, Mass. 1966); R.S.Thorn 'The Evolution of Public Finances during Economic Development' *Manchester School* January 1967; J.R.Lotz and E.R.Morss 'Measuring "Tax Effort" in Developing Countries' *I.M.F. Staff Papers* November 1967.

9 It would clearly be even better if the standardisation procedure could be carried further, e.g. by adjustment for differences and density of population

10 *U.N. Statistical Yearbook 1966* (New York 1967)

11 There were so few countries in the under $2\frac{1}{2}$ million class that any comparison would have been meaningless.

13 It may be worth noting that of three countries with a measure of similarity in background, income levels, etc. – India, Pakistan and Ceylon – the ratios were found to be 27 per cent, 31 per cent and 71 per cent respectively. In this case there is a very clear difference between the smaller country and the larger ones.

14 Oka Orewa *Taxation in Western Nigeria* (Oxford 1962)

15 It would be argued that the case of Nigeria is contrary to what one would expect on the basis of our *a priori* conjectures in that one has a variety of income tax systems even within a federal structure. But it can be countered that a federal structure is a necessary, if not a sufficient, condition for avoiding such problems.

16 A.Adedeji 'The Future of Personal Income Taxation in 1965' *Nigerian Journal of Economic and Social Studies* July 1965.

17 See e.g. *Statistical Yearbook 1966*, tables on public finances.

18 *Report*, Cmnd. 1164 (HMSO, October 1960) p. 72.

19 *Evidence of Rural District Councils Association* 1966

20 This point is very relevant to the situation of Nigeria in 1968, with the prospect of 13 major administrations (Federal Government plus 12 states) instead of 5.

21 Institute of Municipal Treasurers and Accountants *Police Force Statistics* 1966/67 (London, January 1968)

22 H. J. Kiesling 'Measuring a Local Government Service; a Study of School Districts in New York State' *Review of Economics and Statistics* August 1967.

23 It might be noted the UK formulae for central government grants to local authorities have never had any components based on economies of scale.

S. HYMER AND S. RESNICK

Interactions Between the Government and the Private Sector : an Analysis of Government Expenditure Policy and the Reflection Ratio

I. INTRODUCTION

Theoretical models of underdeveloped countries often draw policy conclusions concerning various development strategies without explicitly taking into account the role of the government. The focus is usually on the relationship between agriculture and industry rather than between the private and public sectors. Yet to ignore the specific contribution of the government as a provider of crucial development inputs or to fail to consider the government as a decision maker having its own set of preferences is to omit an important part of the development model. The purpose of this paper is to introduce the government as a sector having its own set of objectives, instruments, and constraints and to explore the resulting interactions between the government and the private sector.

There are a number of important characteristics of the government sector in underdeveloped countries that deserve special attention. First, a significant share of government activity in developing countries has a directly productive effect on other sectors of the economy. Government financed infrastructure and education, for example, often form a major part of the physical and human capital stock of the country. Government services in transportation, communications, research, peace and order, etc. are intermediate goods which affect the level of productivity in the private sector. Expenditure policy is thus a crucial instrument of development strategy.

Secondly, the capacity of the government to earn revenue is limited severely by the costs of collecting taxes and by political and ideological constraints on the tax structure. In many underdeveloped countries, the largest share of revenue is derived from indirect taxes on a limited number of exported or imported commodities. The revenue of the government depends therefore upon the growth of taxable sectors.

Finally, the government sector can appropriately be viewed as an institution within society having its own goals and preferences some of which may be in harmony with the objectives of the private sector and some of which may be in conflict. These goals are determined by the specific political process of the country and reflect the interests and power of various pressure groups as well as the desires of the state bureaucracy and ambitions of the ruling *élite*. In technical terms, we cannot assume the government is in all cases attempting to achieve Pareto efficiency for the country as a whole but instead we must view the government as maximizing specific goals of its own subject to specific constraints.[1]

These principles of productive expenditure, limited tax capacity, and specific government preference functions, taken together, imply a quasi-market mechanism to determine the growth of the government sector and its impact on the private sector. If government expenditure policies fail to stimulate the growth of the economy, and in particular those sectors from which it derives its taxes, government revenue ceases to grow, and its expansion must come to a halt. For survival and growth, the government must allocate some of its resources in directions that will generate income. This, however, sets limits on government behaviour within which it chooses according to its preference function.

The reflection ratios

Formally, we may derive the relevant relationship between the private and public sectors as follows. The size of the government sector is constrained by its budget equation

$$G = R + B \tag{1.1}$$

where G equals total expenditures, R total revenue and B net borrowing. Ignoring B for the moment, the size of G and its rate of growth through time depends upon the level and rate of growth of R. The point of departure for this article is that there is a functional dependence of R upon G which may be called the reflection ratio.

Our first principle noted above says that the level of activity of various sectors of the economy is functionally related to the expenditure policy of the government. This relationship can be written as

$$X = F(g) \tag{1.2}$$

where X is a vector of indices of economic private economic activity, and g a government expenditure vector whose elements $(g_1, g_2, ..., g_n)$ denote the level of activity of a particular government function.[2]

The second principle states that government revenue will depend upon the vector of private economic activities

$$R = tX \tag{1.3}$$

where R equals total revenue and t is a tax vector whose elements are the given tax rates associated with each private economic activity. We assume for this paper that the tax structure represented by this vector tends to be stable over time. Our primary concern is to analyse the effect of changing g, given t as a constraint. In underdeveloped countries, it can reasonably be argued that governments have only limited scope for changing t within a given economic structure. In the short run it can thus be viewed as exogenous. An analysis of changes in t, especially the discontinuous jumps that occur with economic revolution, is beyond the scope of the present paper. [3]

Combining these equations we obtain the reflection ratio

$$G = tF(g) + B \tag{1.4}$$

which indicates that the level of government expenditures is functionally determined by its composition.

Another type of reflection ratio can be devised as follows. The government sector requires certain inputs from the rest of the economy, e.g., imported goods, labour, raw materials, etc. But government expenditure influences the supply curve of these inputs. Government help to export industries, for example, increases the supply of foreign exchange, while government help to agriculture lowers the price of food and hence the supply price of labour and intermediate goods, and government expenditure on education increases the supply of skilled personnel. These relationships generate a second type of feedback of government expenditure on government expenditure.

This general relationship between governmental inputs and its own expenditure can be illustrated in the following simple model. Assume the government uses only one factor of production, labour (L), and the amount it can employ is equal to total revenue (R) divided by the wage rate (w). If we define the productivity of each worker as a, the total output of the government sector is then given by

$$G = \frac{a}{w}R. \text{[4]} \tag{1.5}$$

A certain portion of total government expenditure, say g_2, is assumed to have a direct effect on either the productivity of government labour (a) or its cost (w). The second type of reflection ratio can then be derived as

$$\frac{a}{w} = \rho(g_2). \tag{1.6}$$

A Model of the Two Types of Reflection Ratios

We can now summarize our basic relationship between the private and public sectors in the following simplified set of equations:[5]

$$G = \frac{a}{w} R \tag{2.1}$$

$$g_0 = G - g_1 - g_2 \tag{2.2}$$

$$R = \rho_1(g_1) \tag{2.3}$$

$$\frac{a}{w} = \rho_2(g_2). \tag{2.4}$$

Equation (2.2) states that government activity can be divided into three kinds: g_0 which has no directly productive effect on the economy in the period under consideration but is either a government consumption item or a long range development activity; g_1 which has a direct effect on output in the private sector and hence on the government's revenue as described by equation (2.3); and g_2 which has a direct effect on either the productivity of labour in the government sector or its cost (equation (2.4)). The total output of the government as given by (2.1) can then be rewritten as

$$G = \rho_2(g_2)\, \rho_1(g_1).$$

This model can be seen schematically in figure 1, which demonstrates the two feedback loops from government expenditure to government expenditure. This illustrates, for example, that even if the government is interested in maximizing development expenditure such as g_0, it must spend certain sums on g_1 and g_2 because of their indirect effects in producing g_0.

II. THE GOVERNMENT'S CHOICE

The problem confronting the government in choosing the optimal level and allocation of expenditure is illustrated in figure 2. For the present we are considering only the first type of reflection ratio, i.e., ρ_1 or the feedback from increased tax revenue. As before, B is set equal to zero. It is further assumed in the background that there are three sectors: X_1, a taxed export or manufacturing sector; X_2, a non-taxed large agrarian and service sector which supplies an unlimited amount of labour at a constant wage; and G, the government sector whose activity affects X_1.

The reflection curve is pictured in quadrant I which shows the total level of government expenditure as a function of the amount allocated to g_1. It is derived as follows:

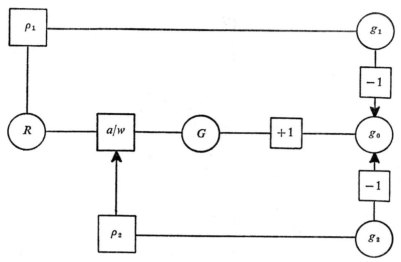

Model:

$$G = \frac{a}{w} R \qquad\qquad R = \rho_1(g_1)$$

$$g_0 = G - g_1 - g_2 \qquad\qquad \frac{a}{w} = \rho_2(g_2)$$

Figure 1   Two feedback loops from G onto G

Quadrant IV shows the productivity of the government on the private sector according to $X_1 = F(g_1)$ where the curve is concave downward due to diminishing returns, $F' > 0$, $F'' < 0$. If the government set $g_1 = 0$, it is assumed that the level of private output would be $X_1 = \bar{X}_1$.

Quadrant III indicates the relationship between activity in the private sector and the tax revenue of the government. We have assumed taxes are a constant proportion of activity in X_1 but could easily explore the case where taxes are an increasing or decreasing proportion. It should be noted that we have assumed that taxes have no disincentive effect on production. This is not realistic but could be relaxed by making the revenue function concave to the X_1 axis thereby changing the shape of the reflection curve in the first quadrant.

The second quadrant shows the relationship between revenue and government expenditure. Assuming a balanced budget, $R = G$, the relationship is a straight line with a 45° slope.

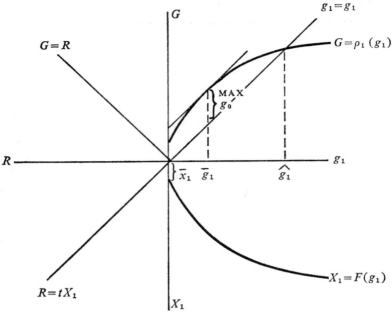

Model:

$X_1 = F(g_1)$ Productivity of government $(F' > 0, F'' < 0)$

$R = tX_1$ Revenue function

$R = G$ Balanced budget $(B = 0)$

$G = \rho_1(g_1)$ Reflection curve $(\rho_2 = 0)$

Figure 2   The government's choice

The reflection curve in quadrant I tells us the total amount of government expenditure associated with any level of expenditure on g_1. It is derived by choosing various initial levels of g_1 which determine X_1, then R, and finally back onto G.[6] The horizontal difference between the reflection curve and a 45° line indicates the surplus available to the government for expenditure on $g_0 (g_0 = \rho_1(g_1) - g_1)$.

What is the optimum point for the government? It is immediately evident that there is no obvious single best point in the absence of a social welfare function to evaluate the desirabilities of various combinations of government and private activity. Thus we must introduce our third principle of government behaviour. It is unrealistic to assume that the government in underdeveloped countries always maximizes some vague notion of 'general welfare' representing somehow the combined interests and views of the population as a whole. It is also unrealistic to assume that the government always strives to achieve Pareto optimality and then redistributes using lump sum taxes and transfers. A particular government is pushed and pulled by its own views of the world and by political pressures of various groups both internal and external. We assume instead that the government (i.e. the state) in an underdeveloped country has its own welfare function possibly different from a large section of the private sector. It is appropriate, therefore, to analyse problems in terms of the implications and contradictions of various possible social welfare functions.

Suppose we make the crude assumption that the government's only interest is g_0. The X_1 sector, for example, may be a foreign firm operating in the export sector of no interest to the government except for the revenue it provides through taxes which can then be spent on armies, monuments, or development. The government would then choose the point $\bar{g}_1$, where g_0 is a maximum. [7]

Another crude assumption, with quite different effects, is that the government's only interest is in its total size. It may, for example, try to maximize G regardless of composition because of the employment generating aspects. The government would then choose the point $\bar{g}_1$ where g_0 is equal to zero. This is the point which maximizes the total size of X_1 as well because of the particular assumptions of this model. A government choosing this policy would therefore obtain the largest possible combined employment in the export plus government sector, at the expense of the rest of the economy if g_0 were considered to be partly development expenditures with a long gestation period.

In figure 3, we can summarize the various distributions between g_0 and g_1 (quadrant I) from the government's point of view. A social welfare function, $U(g_0, g_1)$ is drawn to indicate one possible solution equating the marginal rates of substitution and transformation. Our two limiting points, A and B, are indicated to show the range of the government's choice.

Neither of these extremes, however, is sufficient to describe government behaviour in a complex world. In actual fact, the government will assign utility weights to a number of objectives: employment, output, size of the private sector, degree of openness of the economy, etc. The proposition remains empirically empty as long as we do not know the content of the government's preference function. Nonetheless, the above analysis contains an important lesson for research on the structure and performance of economies and the evaluation of national income. The economic record of a country does not merely reflect technological production functions and factor

M

supplies but also the tastes of the government. Models which omit this latter feature, and this is the case in most theoretical and empirical models of underdeveloped countries, are therefore misspecified to the extent that the government sector is an important force in the economy.

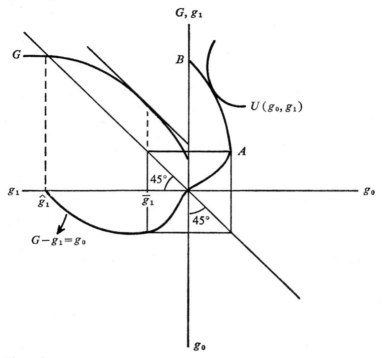

Figure 3

III. A BARGAINING MODEL

The reflection ratio as derived in the preceding sections focuses on the allocation of government expenditure solely from the point of view of the government itself. For a given tax rate, the government surplus g_0, rose to a maximum and then fell as increasing amounts were spent on 'productive' activities, g_1 or g_2. Given the government's preference function, we were able to indicate the choice of the policy instrument, g_0, which maximized the government's objective function.

The government, however, does not act in a vacuum since its choice of expenditure policy has a direct effect on output and profits in the private sector. A simple bargaining model, taking into account the preferences of the private sector, can illustrate the regions of conflict and complementarity between the government and the private sector in the choice of policy instruments.

In figure 4, we have drawn an opportunity locus or bargaining curve between various combinations of the private surplus (net of taxes), $\hat{\pi}$, and public surplus, g_0. It is obvious from our preceding analysis that variations in t and g_1 will affect the surplus of both the government and private sector. If the economy is within the frontier, say at point A, then a change in t or g_1 will make both sectors better off by moving to, say, point B on the frontier. There is then a complementary relationship between the two surpluses for given changes in t or g_1. Once at point B, however, a trade-off between private and public surplus exists and a potential movement to point C must involve us with a political bargaining process or the specification of a social welfare function, $U(g_0, \hat{\pi})$, for the entire economy. In the following discussion, we will derive this opportunity locus and provide some possible reasons why certain underdeveloped countries might end up within the frontier.

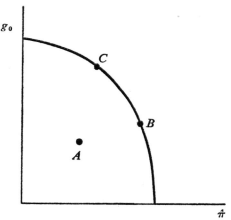

Figure 4   Opportunity locus between private and public sectors

The bargaining model is characterized by two equations relating the government surplus (g_0) and the private surplus ($\hat{\pi}$) to the two policy instruments, the rate of tax on profits (t) and the level of productive expenditure (g_1). The government surplus is defined as the excess of revenue over expenditure on g_1 and the private surplus as after tax profits:

(i) government surplus equation $g_0 = t\pi - g_1$

(ii) private surplus equation $\hat{\pi} = (1-t)\pi$

where the range of the variables is restricted so that t lies between 0 and 1, and g_0 is always positive.

The family of government *iso-surplus curves* will be U-shaped as pictured in figure 5 (the diagram has been drawn to scale using specific analytical functions described in the appendix). The slope of this curve is defined as follows:

$$\frac{dt}{dg_1} = -\frac{\dfrac{\partial g_0}{\partial g_1}}{\dfrac{\partial g_0}{\partial t}}$$

The denominator of this expression, $\partial g_0/\partial t$, is always positive since for a given expenditure on g_1, an increase in the tax rate will increase revenue and hence the government surplus. The numerator is positive for low values of g_1 and then becomes negative. As we saw in figure 2, the government surplus at first increases for a given tax rate as more is spent on g_1, but then decreases after the point where the marginal productivity of g_1 ($\partial \pi / \partial g_1$) falls below $1/t$. This can be shown algebraically from equation (i):

$$\frac{\partial g_0}{\partial g_1} = t\frac{\partial \pi}{\partial g_1} - 1$$

$$\therefore \frac{\partial g_0}{\partial g_1} \lessgtr 0 \text{ as } \frac{\partial \pi}{\partial g_1} \lessgtr \frac{1}{t}.$$

It should be noted in figure 5 that the turning point occurs at large values of g_0 the higher is t. The shape of the *iso government surplus curve* is thus negative and then positive as the numerator changes sign with increasing g_1. The turning point shifts upward and to the right for higher *iso government surplus curves* (the reader is again referred to the appendix for a formal derivation using specific analytical functions).

The *iso-profit curve* is much simpler to derive because an increase in g_1 always has a positive effect on profits after tax while an increase in t always has a negative effect. The slope of the *iso-profit curve* is therefore always positive (see figure 6)[8]

$$\frac{dt}{dg_1} - \frac{\dfrac{\partial \hat{\pi}}{\partial g_1}}{\dfrac{\partial \hat{\pi}}{\partial t}} \cdot$$

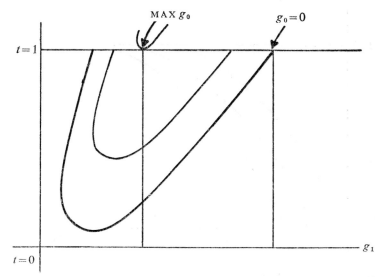

Figure 5   Iso-surplus curves

The *iso government surplus curve* and the *iso-profit curve* can be superimposed on an Edgeworth Bowley-type diagram (figure 7). The tangencies of *iso-profit* and *iso-surplus curves* yield a contract curve showing the trade-off between $\hat{\pi}$ and g_0 with optimal combinations of t and g_1. If we map the points on this contract curve onto a $\{\hat{\pi}, g_0\}$ space, we then derive the opportunity locus as in figure 4.

A theory of bargaining as well as a theory of politics would be necessary to predict the eventual resting point. We may for the moment confine ourselves to one case to illustrate that many countries may not be on the contract curve.

Suppose we begin with a given tax rate t. The government's expenditure policy is then a straight line parallel to the g_1 axis and perpendicular to the t axis. As g_1 increases, g_0 increases up to point A and $\hat{\pi}$ increases up to point B which is beyond A. Suppose the government chooses to maximize g_0 by resting at A. It is obvious that both parties could be made better off by increasing t and g_1 in some combination that moves the economy to the contract curve. Will such a move necessarily occur? The private sector may very well resist it. It may prefer a lazy incompetent government to an efficient one. An efficient government would move to the contract curve but, once there, might decide to move along it by squeezing profits. It may be in the private sector's interest to keep the government as a

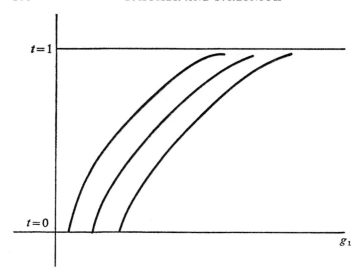

Figure 6   Iso-profit curves

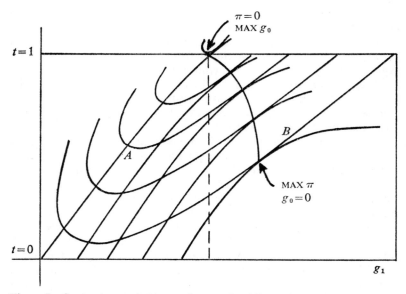

Figure 7   Contract curve between private and public sectors

satisficer by giving it enough g_0 to keep it stable and content, even though this sacrifices efficiency.

This simple analysis covers only two variables. In the real world, the government would no doubt be interested in other targets (employment, output, etc.). These also vary as g_1 varies. A specification of social welfare functions would be necessary to analyse the more complex case. For the moment we may merely note that the derivatives dX_1/dg_1, dL/dg_1, etc. all have different values and there is no unique maximum for the society.

IV. A DYNAMIC MODEL

Movements along the efficiency frontier for g_0 and $\hat{\pi}$ have important dynamic implications which should be taken into account when choosing the appropriate government fiscal policy. Profits are one of the major sources of private savings in underdeveloped countries and the level of $\hat{\pi}$ becomes an important determinant of the rate of private capital formation. In a similar vein, the government uses some part of its surplus, g_0, for capital formation and development. A particular combination of $\hat{\pi}$ and $\hat{g}_0$ in one period determines the level and mix of private and public investment and hence the rate of growth of the economy.

Suppose, for example, government investment is zero and that the

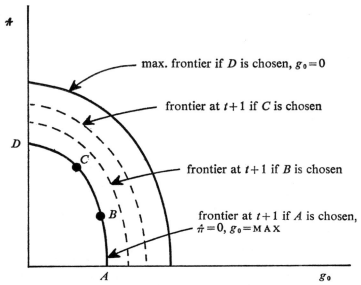

Figure 8   Efficiency frontier for g_0 and $\hat{\pi}$

private sector reinvests some fraction s_1 of its net profits. The greater the level of $\hat{\pi}$ permitted the private sector, the greater the rate of capital formation and hence the greater the *outward shift in the efficiency frontier*. This is illustrated in figure 8 which shows the efficiency frontier of period $t+1$ corresponding to a choice of point A, B, C, or D in period t. If point A is chosen so that $\hat{\pi}=0$ and g_0 is a maximum, no capital formation occurs and the efficiency frontier remains stationary. If point D is chosen so that g_0 is zero and $\hat{\pi}$ a maximum, the efficiency frontier shifts to the maximum possible extent. B and C are intermediate choices.

The government's choice of g_0 in one period thus affects its possibility of choice in the next period and so on *ad infinitum*. The optimum choice from the government's point of view depends upon its horizon and time preference. Suppose, for example, the government's time horizon extends only one period and it derives no utility from $\hat{\pi}$. We assume then that at $t+1$ the government will choose the point where $\hat{\pi}(t+1)=0$ and $g_0(t+1)$ is a maximum. A one period Fisher production possibilities curve can then be derived from figure 8 showing for each g_0 at time t, the amount of g_0 obtainable at $t+1$:[9]

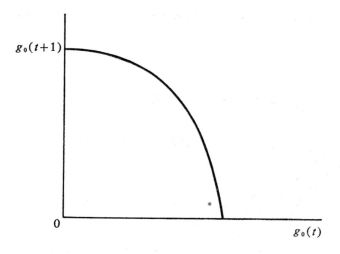

A more interesting model allows both the public and private sectors to contribute to capital formation. There are two types of capital stock used by the private sector: K_1 which is the private capital stock consisting of plant, equipment, etc., and K_2 which is the public capital stock consisting of infrastructure, human capital, etc. Private investment is a function of profits and public investment is a function of revenue. The basic model is as follows:

$$Y = F(K_1, K_2, L)\,{}^{10} \tag{3.1}$$

$$I_1 = s\hat{\pi} = s(1-t)\pi \tag{3.2}$$

$$I_2 = g\,t\,\pi \tag{3.3}$$

$$g_0 = G - I_2 \tag{3.4}$$

where:

Y = total private output
K_1 = private capital stock
K_2 = public capital stock
L = labour employed in Y
I_1 = private investment
I_2 = public investment
s = private savings rate
g = government savings rate
t = tax rate on profits (π)
$\hat{\pi}$ = private profits net of taxes
g_0 = public surplus
G = total government expenditure

Differentiating (3.1) totally, we have

$$dY = f_1\,dK_1 + f_2\,dK_2 + f_3\,dL \tag{3.5}$$

but $dK_1 = I_1$, $dK_2 = I_2$ and $f_3 = w$ where w is the wage rate assumed given (i.e., we assume a perfectly elastic supply of labour at the given w).[11] (3.5) can then be rewritten as

$$dY - w\,dL = f_1\,I_1 + f_2\,I_2, \tag{3.6}$$

$$\text{or } d\pi = f_1\,s(1-t)\pi + f_2 g\,t\pi \tag{3.7}$$

where we have used equations (3.2) and (3.3).

(3.7) can be converted into a growth equation showing the rate of growth of private profits in terms of the two instrumental variables, t and g, as follows:

$$\frac{d\pi}{\pi} = \pi^* = f_1 s(1-t) + f_2 g t. \tag{3.8}$$

The government, however, is interested in its surplus g_0. There is then a relationship between π^* and the relative public private surplus ratio g_0/π as follows:

By definition, $g_0 = (1-g)t\pi$ where $t\pi = G$ (see equation (3.4)), and $gt = t - g_0/\pi$. Substituting this into the growth equation (3.8) we have

$$\pi^* = f_1 s(1-t) + f_2 (t - \frac{g_0}{\pi}). \tag{3.9}$$

For a given t, $\pi^* = F\left(\dfrac{g_0}{\pi}\right)$ where $\dfrac{\partial \pi^*}{\partial \dfrac{g_0}{\pi}} < 0$.

These growth equations can be used to illustrate the growth paths associated with different levels of the instrumental variables g and t. To anticipate our results, the model shows that the government must choose among growth paths such as the ones depicted in figure 9. Path A has a higher initial level of g_0 than path B but a lower rate of growth. Path B sacrifices present g_0 but generates a higher rate of growth given a higher initial g or lower t than path A.

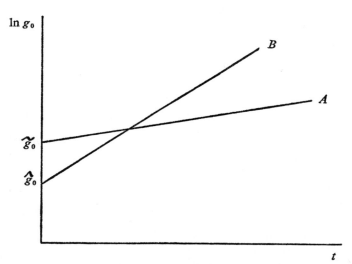

Path A: higher initial $\hat{g}_0$ but lower rate of growth.
Path B: sacrifice present $\hat{g}_0$ but higher rate of growth as higher initial g_1 or lower t.
If g_0 is spent only on consumption, then problem is only of time preference:

$$\text{MAX} \int_0^\infty V(g_0)dt \text{ subject to } g_0^* = f(g_0 t).$$

Figure 9   Alternative paths of g_0

Let us now turn to the derivation of the government's decision rules for a given g_0/π. Differentiating equation (3.9) partially with respect to t reveals that for a given g_0/π the growth rate of π and g_0 rises or falls as t increases depending on whether $f_1 s \lesseqgtr f_2$, or

$$\frac{\partial \pi^*}{\partial t} = -f_1 s + f_2, \qquad (4.0)$$

where $\partial \pi^*/\partial t \lesseqgtr 0$ as $f_1 s \lesseqgtr f_2$.

This result can be given a straightforward interpretation. f_2 is the productivity of a dollar's worth of investment in public capital formation. $f_1 s$ is the productivity of a dollar's worth of tax reduction to the private sector taking into account both the productivity of private capital and the leakage into private consumption. For a given level of g_0, the government will wish to have all capital formation taking place either in K_1 or K_2 depending upon whether $f_1 s \gtrless f_2$.

We can summarize the results of this model in the following two decision rules:

Case 1. If $f_2 > f_1 s$, the government sets t at a maximum, i.e. equal to 1, thus reducing private investment to zero. The growth equation then becomes

$$\pi^* = f_2 \left(1 - \frac{g_0}{\pi} \right).$$

The higher the level of g_0 the lower the rate of growth of π^* and hence of g_0.

Case 2. If $f_1 s > f_2$, the government sets public capital formation at zero and raises taxes only for g_0, i.e., $t = g_0/\pi$. The growth equation then becomes

$$\pi^* = f_1 s \left(1 - \frac{g_0}{\pi} \right)$$

and again there is a trade-off between the share of profits devoted to g_0 and the rate of growth, the higher the t the lower the rate of growth.

These two cases, however, illustrate only partial solutions, since they assume $f_1 s$ and f_2 will remain constant over time. In fact, they will vary as the ratio of K_1/K_2 changes. In case 1, $K_1^* = 0$ and $K_2^* > 0$, hence K_1/K_2 will fall and $f_1 s/f_2$ will rise until $f_1 s = f_2$. In case 2, $K_2^* = 0$ and $K_1 > 0$, therefore K_1/K_2 rises and $f_1 s/f_2$ will fall.

The equilibrium growth path will always, therefore, tend to what we call case 3 where $f_1 s = f_2$. Along the equilibrium growth path, K_1/K_2 will equal $\overline{K}^*$, the particular public private capital ratio which equates $f_1 s$ to f_2. The ratio of I_1 to I_2 will also have to be equal to $\overline{K}^*$

to maintain the growth path. We can then solve for t along this equilibrium path as follows:

Solving (3.9) for the equilibrium growth rate yields

$$\bar{K} = \frac{(1-t)}{\left(t - \frac{g_0}{\pi}\right)}.$$

Therefore, $t = \dfrac{1 + \bar{K} \cdot \dfrac{g_0}{\pi}}{(1 + \bar{K})}.$

Our major conclusion from this model, that the government must choose between g_0/π and π^*, still holds. This can easily be seen by once again turning to equation (3.9) and letting $f_1 s = f_2$ for equilibrium. This yields

$$\pi^* = f_2\left(1 - t + t - \frac{g_0}{\pi}\right) = f_1 s\left(1 - t + t - \frac{g_0}{\pi}\right)$$

$$= f_2\left(1 - \frac{g_0}{\pi}\right) = f_1 s\left(1 - \frac{g_0}{\pi}\right)$$

and the government's choice between π^* and g_0/π is again evident.

We may now briefly examine some of the factors which enter into the government's choice of growth paths. First, let us suppose g_0 is spent entirely on public consumption in the interest of either the nation as a whole or some particular group in control. The optimization problem is then simply one of time preference. Given a time rate of discount, the government can choose the income stream that maximizes the present discounted value of a stream of g_0 with initial value $\bar{g}_0$ and a rate of growth g_0^*.[12]

It is, however, more interesting and relevant to assume that g_0 is used, at least in part, for general developmental purposes or for some other productive activity. Suppose g_0 is used as an investment in another sector Y_2 which will also feed back revenue to the government when it becomes productive. Suppose that this alternate outlet for investment funds has a rate of return of r_2. The flow of funds to the government is now composed of two streams: the first is $g_0 e^{r1 t}$, the surplus generated by the sector Y_1 analysed above; the second stream is $g_0 e^{r2 t}$, the stream generated by investing g_0 in a development program. The funds available to the government at some future point will therefore be:

$$g_0 e^{r1 t} + g_0 e^{r2 t} = g_0(e^{r1 t} + e^{r2 t}).$$

The government will maximize the discounted value of this stream, keeping in mind that r_1 is a declining function of g_0. It is also likely that r_2 will be a declining function of g_0 if there are diminishing returns. A more realistic variant, too complicated to analyse here, is to assume that the development programme has a long gestation period so that for the first n years it yields zero return.

Finally, we explore a model in which the government invests in a capital stock which increases the productivity of labour in the government sector itself. We assume that there is a government production function relating output of the government sector to its own capital stock and to labour employed by the government

$$G = G(K, L).[13] \tag{4.1}$$

Labour is available in unlimited amounts at a fixed wage rate $\bar{w}$. Government investment is the surplus of revenue over wages

$$I = R - \bar{w}L. \tag{4.2}$$

We further assume that R is determined autonomously and grows at a constant rate R^*. A balanced growth path is then defined in which all variables are growing at the same rate:

$$G^* = K^* = L^* = I^* = R^*.$$

In this model, the government's instrumental variable is its savings rate, i.e., the fraction of total revenue in each period which it devotes to its own investment. The choice is illustrated in figure 10 for arbitrary levels of R. We assume that the government chooses an expansion path implying a constant savings rate I/R. It is easy to show that given an exogenously determined rate of growth of R, there is one optimum savings rate that provides the highest possible growth path for G. There exists then a golden rule for government investment along a balanced growth path equal to R^* which is the analogue to the natural growth rate.

We know that along the balanced growth path, capital grows at the same rate as revenue or $I = KR^*$. Substituting this in equation (4.2) above, we obtain for any point of time

$$R = R^* K + \bar{w}L. \tag{4.3}$$

This equation provides the government with the opportunity cost of capital and labour. The government can vary its capital labour ratio by varying its savings rate as long as it satisfies equation (4.3).

The problem for the government is to choose the K and L which maximizes G (equation (4.1)) subject to the constraint that $R = R^* K + \bar{w}L$. The solution is illustrated graphically in figure 11. The maximum occurs where the ratio of the marginal productivity of

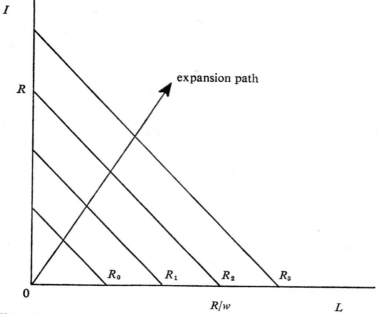

Figure 10

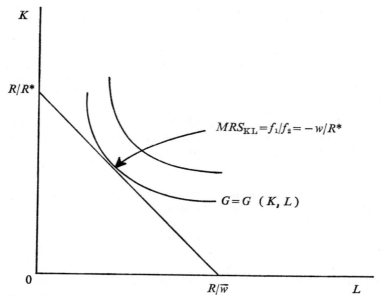

Figure 11

labour and capital, f_1/f_2, equals $-w/R$. This is the golden rule for the government.

It is interesting to relate this to other formulations of the golden rule. By Euler's theorem,

$$G = f_1 L + f_2 K.$$

and by equation (4.3) above,

$$R = \bar{w}L + R^* K.$$

Suppose we assume that we can convert the government's equation to monetary terms by multiplying through by P_g such that $P_g G = R$. In other words, we assume (as is the usual practice) that the value of government output is equal to the value of total revenue and to expenditure by the government in investment and on labour. Our equations would then read:

$$P_g G = P_g f_1 L + P_g f_2 K$$
$$R = \bar{w}L + R^* K.$$

Since $\dfrac{f_1}{f_2} = \dfrac{w}{R^*}$, we conclude that

$$w = P_g f_1$$
$$R^* = P_g f_2.$$

Along the golden rule path, the marginal revenue product of capital equals the growth rate and the marginal revenue product of labour equals the wage rate. It is important to note that in order to obtain this result, we assumed that the value of government output in any year equalled the value of current expenditures plus capital expenditures. The true definition of total value should be current expenditure, $\bar{w}L$, plus imputed capital costs. Our formula requires the assumption that capital costs should be imputed at the rate of growth R^*

APPENDIX TO SECTION III

The bargaining model can be written as follows (definition of variables are found in the text):

$$X_1 = g_1{}^\alpha L^\beta K^\gamma \tag{1}$$

$$K = \bar{K} \tag{2}$$

$$w = \frac{\beta X_1 P}{L} \tag{3}$$

$$R = t\pi = t(1-\beta)X_1 \tag{4}$$

$$\hat{\pi} = (1-t)\pi \tag{5}$$

$$R = G = g_0 + g_1 \tag{6}$$

Equation (1) describes the production function for the private sector. It is assumed to be Cobb-Douglas. In this production function, the effect of g_1 is like neutral technological change in the sense that it does not affect the marginal rates of substitution between K and L. For many purposes, it would be more interesting and relevant to explore the possibility that government expenditure on, say, research or education is biased towards capital or labour. Note that g_1 is assumed to be a flow whereas many government activites, e.g., roads and dams are better viewed as a capital stock. The model might be viewed as describing periods of time longer than one year, or if viewed as a short-run model, as covering only the recurrent expenditure of government on maintaining roads, providing information, etc.

Equation (2) assumes that the private capital is fixed in the period of consideration.

Equation (3) indicates that labour is hired up to the point where the wage rate equals the marginal product. Because of the Cobb-Douglas assumption and the assumption of constant wages and prices, this yields an expression for labour as a simple non-linear function of X_1:

$$L = \frac{P\beta}{w} X_1$$

Equation (4) shows total revenue for the government (equal to total expenditure) as a constant ratio of profits. Profits before tax is the residual after paying wages and because of the Cobb-Douglas assumption is a constant share of output.

Equations (5) and (6) derive respectively profits after tax $(\hat{\pi})$ and total R and G.

Solving equations 1 – 6 in terms of g_1:

$$X_1 = Ag_1^\lambda \tag{7}$$
$$L = Bg_1^\lambda \tag{8}$$
$$R = tCg_1^\lambda \tag{9}$$
$$\hat{\pi} = (1-t)Cg_1^\lambda \tag{10}$$
$$g_0 = tCg_1^\lambda - g_1 \tag{11}$$

where $A = \left(\dfrac{P\beta}{w}\right)^{\frac{\beta}{1-\beta}} K^{\frac{\alpha}{1-\beta}}$

$\lambda = \dfrac{\alpha}{1-\beta}$ and $\dfrac{\alpha}{1-\beta} < 1$ since $\alpha + \beta < 1$

$B = \dfrac{P\beta}{w} A$

$C = (1-\beta)A$

Derivation of iso-surplus curves

$$g_0 = tCg_1^\lambda - g_1$$

$$t = \frac{g_0}{Cg_1^\lambda} + \frac{g_1}{Cg_1^\lambda}$$

$$\frac{dt}{dg_1} = g_1^{-\lambda} \left[\frac{-\lambda g_0}{Cg_1} + \frac{(1-\lambda)}{C} \right]$$

$$\frac{dt}{dg_1} \lessgtr 0 \text{ as } g_1 \lessgtr \frac{\lambda g_0}{(1-\lambda)}$$

Given b_0,

$$\underset{g_1 \to 0}{\text{LIM } t} = +\infty \text{ and } \underset{g_1 \to \infty}{\text{LIM } t} = +\infty$$

If $t = 1$, $g_0 = 0$ when $g_1 = C^{\frac{1}{1-\lambda}}$

For MAX g_0, $\dfrac{dg_0}{dg_1} = \lambda tcg_1^{\lambda-1} - 1 = 0$

and when $t = 1$, $g_0 = $ MAX

when $g_1 = (\lambda C)^{\frac{1}{1-\lambda}}$

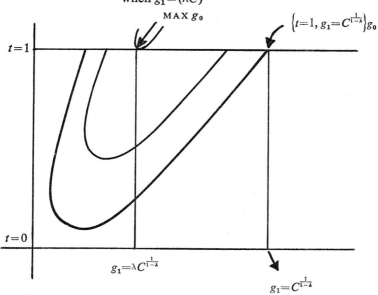

Family of U-shaped curves whose maximum point shifts upward to right as b_0 increases, and is at maximum when $g_1 = \lambda C^{\frac{1}{1-\lambda}}$; lower bound is shown where $g_0 = 0$, in heavy line.

Figure 5A   Iso-surplus curves

Derivation of iso-profit curves

$$\hat{\pi} = (1-t)Cg_1^\lambda$$

$$t = 1 - \frac{\pi}{Cg_1}\lambda$$

$$\frac{dt}{dg_1} = \lambda\pi C^{-1}g_1^{-\lambda-1} = \frac{\lambda\pi}{Cg_1^{\lambda+1}} > 0$$

$$\frac{d^2t}{dg_1^2} = (-\lambda-1)\lambda\pi/Cg^{\lambda+2} < 0$$

$\therefore$ concave downward.

Given $\hat{\pi}$,

$$\underset{g_1 \to 0}{\text{LIM}}\ t = -\infty \text{ and } \underset{g_1 \to \infty}{\text{LIM}}\ t = 1$$

If $t = 0$, $g_1 = \left(\dfrac{\pi}{C}\right)^{\frac{1}{\lambda}}$

$t = 1$, $\pi = 0$

$\therefore$ zero profit curves, i.e., the limiting case occurs when either $t=1$ or $g_1=0$ and is of rectangular shape.

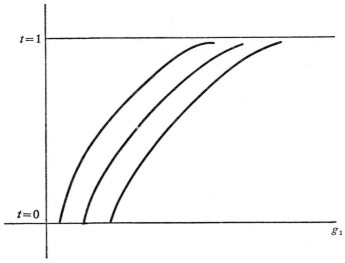

Family of hyperbolas of degree λ concave down where profits increase from left to right; $\pi = 0$ when $t = 1$, or $g_1 = 0$.

Figure 6A   Iso-profit curves

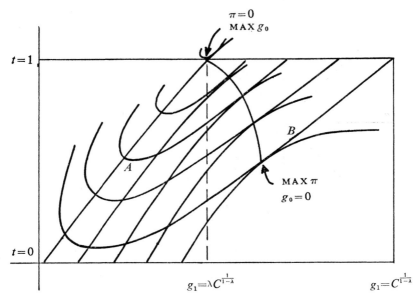

Figure 7A   Contract curve between private and public sectors

The two families can be combined on a single diagram as in figure 7a. The tangencies of *iso-profit* and *iso-surplus* curves yield the contract curve for the specific model in this appendix. As noted, the general case is found in the text.

Notes and references

1 See C. P. Kindleberger, 'Group Behaviour and International Trade'.
2 We assume the following conditions:

$$X = X \text{ if } g = 0, \frac{\partial X}{\partial g} > 0, \overline{\frac{\partial X}{\partial g^2}} < 0.$$

3 Although we are assuming this feature as a stylized fact of underdeveloped countries, considerable empirical estimation remains to be done. This hypothesis implies that a regression of revenue on the level of activity in key sectors would yield stable parameters and a high correlation coefficient over long periods of time. It is to be expected that the structure might shift at given points of time such as when a country moves from colonial to independent status but that it would remain stable within a given period. Data exist for testing this hypothesis, though the relevant investigations have not yet been made.
4 Formally, we may consider the government having a cost contraint $R = wL$ and a production relationship $G = aL$. Solving we derive (1.5).
5 We have ignored net borrowing of the government (B) in this model.
6 Given our assumptions, the reflection curve is the mirror image of the productivity function in quadrant IV, or $\rho_1' > 0$, $\rho_1'' < 0$, and $G = \overline{G}$ when

$g_1=0$. We may also note that our second type of reflection relationship $a/w=\rho_2(g_2)$, could be derived in a somewhat similar manner given $\bar{R}$ as in the following diagram:

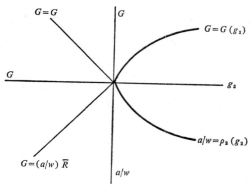

7 $g_0=\rho_1(g_1)-g_1$

g_0 is at a maximum when $\dfrac{dg_0}{dg_1}=1$ or when $g_1=\bar{g}_1$.

8 From equation (ii), we have $d\hat{\pi}=\dfrac{\partial\hat{\pi}}{\partial g_1}dg_1+\dfrac{\partial\hat{\pi}}{\partial t}dt$

$$=(1-t)\dfrac{\partial\pi}{\partial g_1}dg_1-\pi\,dt$$

Setting $d\hat{\pi}=0$ to derive our *iso profit curve*, we have $-\dfrac{(1-t)\dfrac{\partial\hat{\pi}}{\partial g_1}}{-\pi}$

which is clearly positive. Figure 6 is drawn to scale according to the derivation found in the appendix.

9 The well-known formula for deriving the present value of g_0 now and g_0 next period is

$$V=g_0(t)+\dfrac{g_0(t+1)}{(1+i)}$$

where i is the discount rate. This will be maximized when

$$\dfrac{dV}{dg_0}=\dfrac{(1+i)+F'(g_0)}{(1+i)}=0$$

or, $i=-[F'(g_0)+1]$.

10 (3.1) is assumed to be a constant returns to scale production function.
11 The partial derivatives, f_1, indicate the relevant marginal productivities of the private and public capital, and labour.
12 We would calculate the present discounted value of $\int_0^T g_0(0)e^{(g_0*-r)t}dt$

where r is the discount rate, and T the end of the planning period.

Integrating we have $\dfrac{g_0(0)}{g*-r}[e^{(g_0*-r)T}-1]$.

Given that $g_0*=F(\bar{g}_0)$, the maximum could be calculated from the point of view of the government.

13 The government production function is assumed to be a constant returns to scale function.

DAVID WALL

After UNCTAD II

From the point of view of the less developed countries the second session of the United Nations Conference on Trade and Development held in Delhi during February and March 1968 was a failure. The Conference failed to reach decisions for implementation on any of the substantive proposals put forward by either the developed or less developed countries. Issue after issue was resolved by being referred back to committees of the organisation for further research and discussion. This outcome did not surprise observers of the affairs of UNCTAD; it was natural that no progress would be possible while the less developed countries continued to make totally unacceptable demands of the developed countries and while the developed countries were unable to reach agreement on a common position on almost all major issues. To those people who had hoped that UNCTAD would be the forum in which the recognition of the developed countries that the problems of the less developed countries required urgent attention could be translated into action, the *impasse* which has been reached is nothing short of a world tragedy.

An illustration of the extent of this *impasse* is provided by the experience of the UNCTAD world sugar conference which was convened immediately after the Delhi conference had ended. The first week of this conference was completely wasted with discussions as to which country should provide the Vice-Chairman of the Plenary Committee. The second week ended in deadlock when the six countries of the European Economic Community refused to participate in the conference unless they were allowed to be represented as a single negotiating unit; the six EEC delegations resorted to the tactic of walking out of the conference. In such a way is a problem, of fundamental importance to a large group of less developed countries, dealt with in UNCTAD.

Does UNCTAD serve a useful purpose ? The evidence of the first four years of its existence suggests that UNCTAD does serve at least one important purpose. It provides a forum for the discussion of the needs and grievances of the less developed countries. Before the collective criticism of all less developed countries the developed countries have been forced to re-examine their policies in the fields of aid and trade. They have been at some pains to justify their policies, and in some cases promised to amend them. There can be no doubt that in this sense UNCTAD has served a useful purpose and will continue to do so. The role of a forum for critical discussion is a limited one, however, and falls far short of the ambitions that the less developed countries have always had for UNCTAD. They have always hoped that it would develop into a negotiating body designed to formulate treaty binding obligations. This ideal has always been regarded as unrealistic by the developed countries who have taken the line that UNCTAD should be limited to being a discussion centre and that decisions reached should be implemented in other inter-governmental organizations, such as the IMF and GATT.

The decision has been taken to continue UNCTAD as a permanent body of the United Nations Organization. What role will it play? First, it will continue to undertake research into the problems faced by the less developed countries in the international economic environment. No doubt the quality of this work will continue to suffer as a result of the partisan views of many of the people who undertake it. Even so this is an important aspect of UNCTAD's work programme, resulting in the publication of much information which would otherwise be unavailable. In addition, UNCTAD is able to call on the resources of other, less partisan, organizations who have as a result undertaken much important work – such as that of the World Bank on the extent of the export credits problem. In addition it will probably continue to act as a stimulus to research being undertaken by private institutions and individuals.

Second, it will continue to act as an initiator of discussion on issues of concern to the developing countries and to provide an institutional setting for such discussion. The bringing together of experts from many countries to delineate the nature of the development problems falling within the terms of reference of UNCTAD and to evaluate the merits and feasibility of various possible solutions to these problems is an important aspect of the work of UNCTAD. An example of this activity is the Kahn report on international monetary issues.

Third, on the political side, UNCTAD will continue to be the forum in which the attempt is made to reconcile the conflicting positions taken by the different groups of nations on the various recommendations put forward for approval.

On the basis of the decisions reached at Delhi it seems clear that UNCTAD will continue to have the same institutional framework it has had since 1964. Will it be any more successful in using this machinery to achieve its objectives than it has been over the last four years? In view of the current problems besetting the international economic environment it is difficult to give any reply at all to this question, but if the optimist is to give an affirmative answer then it would be on the assumption that two important conditions will be met. First, the preoccupation of the organization with balance of payments problems must give way to a broader treatment of the problems faced by the developing countries. Secondly, the belief that unanimity must be achieved within all groups participating in UNCTAD before progress can be achieved on any issue must be dropped.

It can be expected that the public relations work of UNCTAD in publicizing the balance of payments problems of the less developed countries will continue. But preoccupation with this aspect of development is dangerous. It diverts attention away from the fact that development is primarily a domestic affair, and provides a scapegoat to cover up the incompetences of those responsible for engineering and administrating the development process. Every development economist can recite long lists of examples of chronic waste of foreign exchange in the countries with which he is acquainted. Balance of payments deficits can reflect not only the high cost of development in terms of foreign exchange, but also bad planning – witness the recent experiences of the United Kingdom on this front.

In one sense preoccupation with balance of payments problems is an example of putting the cart before the horse. It results in the merits of the various proposals for changes in the international economic environment being defined in terms of their prospective contributions to the foreign exchange income of the less developed countries. The correct way of assessing the merits of such proposals is to consider how they will facilitate the achievement by the developing countries of their chosen paths to economic development. For example, there has been an extensive debate on the proposal for a generalized scheme of preferences for imports into the developed countries of manufactured and semi-manufactured goods. At no time during the course of this debate in UNCTAD has any consideration been given to the opportunity cost of the factors of production which would have to be diverted from other uses in order to take advantage of the preferences. No thought has been given to the possibility that the nature of the industrialization which the preferences would engender might be inimical to the welfare of the mass of poorer people in the countries receiving the preferences.

Development is primarily a domestic affair, this cannot be repeated often enough and must be taken into account by UNCTAD if its future deliberations are to meet with any success at all. The less developed countries in UNCTAD must show that if the developed countries make concessions in the fields of aid and trade then the resultant increased flows of foreign exchange will be utilized efficiently. This will mean that the developing countries will have to be prepared to indicate how they would use the increased funds which would be made available and, further, be prepared to have such programmes critically examined. It will also mean that they will have to show that they are prepared to make the critical minimum effort of designing, and implementing, efficient and equitable development programmes. The developed countries are simply not prepared to significantly expand the flow of funds to the less developed countries, either through expanded aid programmes or through opening up their markets to increased imports, unless they are assured that such funds will not be wasted.

The second condition which must be satisfied if UNCTAD is to achieve success is the dropping of the myth that schemes are only workable if acceptable to all developed countries as a group. As long as the rate of implementation of proposals depends on the concurrence of the most recalcitant member of the group of developed countries then progress will be very slow indeed. A great deal of time was wasted in Delhi on discussion of whether the developed countries should increase their target for aid from 1 per cent of national income to 1 per cent of gross national income. Much time and effort could have been saved if those countries who were willing from the outset to increase their assistance programmes declared themselves as so being. Similarly, although most developed countries are willing to implement the proposal for a generalized preference system nothing has come of the proposal yet, again because of the unwritten rule that unanimity must be reached before implementation can be effected. What is to stop those countries who are willing to allow imports from developing countries into their markets from doing so unilaterally ? Much is made in this connection of the concept of 'burden sharing', a concept which is both alien to the notions of aid and assistance and empirically meaningless in any case. UNCTAD could usefully take a lesson from the International Monetary Fund on this question. The proposal for a system of Special Drawing Rights has been made subject to implementation on approval by a majority vote, with any country voting against the proposal having the rights to opt out of the operation of the scheme, and to opt in later if they change their mind.

The developed countries seldom, if ever, agree on anything. If such agreement continues to be assumed to be necessary before any proposal made at UNCTAD can be successfully implemented then the efforts of the less developed countries and the work of the Secretariat will continue to be rewarded with failure. Similarly, the developed countries will continue to fail to give serious consideration to any proposal unless they are convinced that the acceptance of such proposals would result in the stimulation of efficient and equitable development.

Index

statement of the problem, 104-5
statistical approximations for
1965, 106-7
World Bank model, 105-6
World Bank report on, 107, 113
Government expenditure
and the reflection ratio, 155-80
characteristics of, in small
countries, 143-5
composition, 151
efficiency, 151-3
the government's choice, 158-62
government intervention, in
supply adjustment, 31, 33

Havana Charter, 42

IBRD, 51
import(s)
as inputs to existing manufacturing industry, 14
expansion, 15
indices of exports and, 36
maintenance, 15
minimum price scheme, 40
of consumer goods, 19-20
prices, separate examination of
export and, 33
providing incentive goods, 14
required, 15, 18-20
restrictions affecting export
prices, 20-1
role in domestic capital
formation, 14
terms of trade and, 36
UN view of, 14-15
import substitution
as the missing component
approach, 7-8, 11-12
criticisms of, 4-7, 11-12
damaging export potential, 22
effect on agriculture, 11
industrialisation and, 6-7, 8
industries set up under, 20
Linder's criteria for, 23-4
manufacturing industry and,
10-11
theory, 3

incentive goods
as inputs to agriculture, 5,
19-20
domestic capital formation for, 14
India
agricultural problems of, 20
cost of living index, 20
devaluation of rupee, 21
failure to promote exports, 22
graduate unemployment in, 9
purchase of consumer imports,
19
shortage of foreign exchange, 17
sugar refining in, 18
varied economy of, 18
industrial
relations, organisation in Kenya,
134-7
unionism, 123
industrialisation
constraints on, 14, 16-17
damaging export potential, 22
definition of, 3, 4, 6
educative value of, 2
export expansion versus
domestic, 1-2
import substitution and, 6-7, 8
in LDCs, foreign trade and,
14, 15
manufacturing industry and, 3
of agriculture, 3
Western techniques in, 19
infant industries
comparative cost structure and,
14-15
inflationary pressures from, 20
protection of, 10
inflation
foreign exchange gap and, 20
of Korean War, 26
instability
and primary producers, 31, 44
effect of devaluation against
dollar, 28-9
MacBean's definition of, 31
or trend in commodities, 28-33
Inter-American Development
Bank, 59-60